D0816562

The
Habsburg Curse

Books by the Same Author

HANS HOLZER

The
Habsburg Curse

DOUBLEDAY & COMPANY, INC., GARDEN CITY, NEW YORK
1973

ISBN: 0-385-02953-5
Library of Congress Catalog Card Number 72–89948
Copyright © 1973 by Hans Holzer
All Rights Reserved
Printed in the United States of America
First Edition

"If the Austrian Empire did not already exist, then it should be created in the interest of Europe, in the interest of mankind even," the Czechoslovak historian Francis Palacky wrote in the middle of the nineteenth century.

He did not say the Habsburg Empire. Austria's historic mission of conciliating the national aspirations of several people in the Danubian area is beyond dispute. But the ruling Habsburg dynasty, up to the last member, at least, considered itself synonymous with the land as if the family owned it and all the people thereon. Now that the Habsburgs rule no more, the head of that ancient family realizes at last that the dynastic mission was an impersonal one and that neither Austria nor Habsburg, but a unified Europe, free and equal in its components, is in the best interest of mankind.

Hans Holzer

New York, New York
June 1972

Contents

Introduction

What exactly is a curse? From time immemorial the belief in curses has existed among men. Strangely enough,
the power of curses is the same as that of blessings. The
ancient terms of malediction and benediction bear witness to the close similarity of the effort involved. It is, of
course, true that the negative is more powerful than the
positive since it involves, at times, great amounts of hatred within the individual performing the magic act
called cursing. To summon similarly strong emotional im-
pacts when blessing an individual is rarely possible.

One of the leading researchers in this area of the occult,
Karl Spiesberger, has pointed out that curses are very real
things. Curses represent thoughts. Thoughts cannot only
create action by their very existence, but are, in fact, also
generating thought forms, which he calls psychogones.

The basic theory behind the effectiveness of curses is
fairly simple. When a person formulates a certain phrase
containing strong emotional expressions of hatred, that
person is, in actuality, creating thought forms that are both
tangible and indestructible. The thought form imbued
with the destructive purpose of the curse is then sent out
either generally or specifically towards one or more in-

dividuals. It is not necessary for the individual, that is to say, the receiver of the curse, to be aware of it. Since the thought form is in itself a tangible thing, it is effective regardless of the receiver's attitude or position. In a sense, then, curses operate somewhat along the lines of dangerous radiation. When a radioactive agent sends forth radioactive emanations, those radioactive particles reach individual human beings and cause certain reactions, frequently damaging. Radioactivity coats objects as well as people and frequently remains in the atmosphere for long periods of time. By the same token, curses simply do not die away but fade very gradually, both electronically when the energy created is dissipated over great stretches of time and emotionally when the original purpose of the curse has been fulfilled. In this respect, then, curses differ greatly from impersonal radiation. This is connected with the basic motivation of the curse which is effective only if the person uttering the curse is truly motivated by strong emotional feelings, generally great hatred, despair or anger. Curses uttered in jest or without true conviction are completely ineffective. That is why any empty phrases containing words like "I'll be damned" or "damn you" are of no significance and do not contain any dangers.

When certain religions prescribe the use of the name of the deity in vain, they do so not because there might be actual damage to the one using God's name without good reason, but purely on dogmatic grounds. Invoking the deity without cause is in violation of proper religious procedure.

Words by themselves are the framework of thought forms. They can differ greatly in their effectiveness according to the mood in which they are uttered. A highly tensed up individual filled with hatred or anger is a most powerful source of electromagnetic energy. That temporarily very strong energy reservoir is condensed by the cursing person into a comparatively small number of words that, in turn, create the thought forms sent forth towards the one for whom the curse is destined. Thus, by compressing a very large psychic force into a very small "container," that container—the curse—becomes very powerful indeed. Spiesberger and other psychic researchers have shown, by citing valid examples, that curses are far from figments of the imagination. They are, in fact, very real energy sources that must be reckoned with. Curses not only direct themselves towards human beings; they can touch animals or even inanimate objects. They can be directed towards entire towns or lands. Curses have been found to be effective against generations of people including many innocent descendants of the original wrong doers.

There are two basic groups of curses. The one uttering the malediction can formulate his curse in general terms or it can be exactly tailored to one individual whom the curser wishes to reach. In the case of the former general group of curses, anyone coming into contact with the accursed person, persons, places or objects will be affected by it. In some cases, general curses are merely protection against unauthorized interference such as with the Egyptian royal tombs.

But there is a third group of curses that is even more powerful than the other two. That is when the one originating the curse is not satisfied with drawing the utmost of his own energies of hatred and anger from the depth of his self and formulating them into words but invokes the powers of darkness as well to support him in his negative quest. This, of course, is done by following certain ritual magical formulas and can be understood or undertaken only by those well versed in the black arts. By combining his own forces with outside energies derived from the psychic world around him, the magician then forges a thunderbolt of hatred that is both extremely effective and difficult to discover. It is even more difficult to counteract.

Nevertheless, there are boundaries beyond which even the most potent curse cannot go. To begin with, any curse reaching its objective and having done what it was meant to do will of itself collapse into nothingness. For example, if a curse has been uttered against a certain family to strike down that family in all its male members, then upon the death of the last heir the curse will disappear.

But beyond this there is the law of karma, which is superior to any curse. If a curse would interfere with the proper karma of an individual, then the curse would be altered or made ineffective. Simply put, if no misdeed has been accomplished yet a curse is uttered against an innocent individual, then that curse will not work. The karmic law requires that every deed be compensated for by another deed. No one need be afraid of being cursed if his conscience is clear. Conversely, if an evil deed has been perpetrated and the perpetrator been cursed, he has every reason to expect the curse to be effective. That, too, is part of the basic karmic law of retribution.

In those cases where the receiver of the curse is made aware of it and wishes to blunt its effectiveness, he has another avenue open. By expressing pure love towards the one who has cursed him, a man can at least influence the effectiveness of the curse. The more love is poured out towards the perpetrator of the curse, the more likely it is to become ineffective. By the same token, if knowledge of an existing curse leads to great anxiety or even an attempt to run away from the curse, this will only result in greater effectiveness of the curse itself.

On the surface at least, the result of successful curses seems to be within the natural law and could, seemingly, be explained by a chain of misfortunes not necessarily connected with each other. Taken in the context of a known curse, they become part and parcel of a deliberate attempt to take revenge on those who have perpetrated a crime in the past and frequently on their descendants. It is with this very real objective in mind that the curse permeating the lives of one of Europe's most distinguished families is being spoken of in the present volume. Some members of that family may deny the existence of that curse, while the majority undoubtedly know nothing about it. Nevertheless, the curse is a reality; it has a basis in fact, and it has indeed found its mark.

The
Habsburg Curse

1 The Mysterious Origin of the Habsburgs

I had heard of the Habsburg curse ever since I was a little boy of eleven. At that time I had been to summer school in Vevey, Switzerland, and my father had sent for me to meet him in Zurich. One of the teachers was elected to accompany me on the train ride. I wasn't exactly his cup of tea. I had been a somewhat iconoclastic pupil during the past weeks, and I have a suspicion he was really glad to get rid of me, but nevertheless, it was going to be a long, hot train ride.

As we were passing through Aargau, the canton or province of Switzerland that lies roughly between Basle and Zurich, Monsieur Koehler, ever the teacher, grabbed my arm suddenly and pointed out the window.

"See that castle over on the hill? That's the old Habsburg."

I looked and in a fleeting glance observed a square tower rising on a hill not too far from the tracks. In a moment the train was past it.

Monsieur Koehler, who had not managed to make too deep an impression on me in class, now took the opportunity to shine before we parted company for good.

"That castle is where the Imperial Habsburgs come

from," he explained, "but very few people realize it.
What's more, did you know the castle is cursed?"

I didn't, although even at that age my curiosity about
such matters was aroused, but Monsieur Koehler knew
very little more.

"*Habsburg* means Hawk Castle, and the story goes that
a man once lived there who was kind to the hawks that
inhabited the grounds. But one day he did something
terribly wrong, and the people of the land put a curse on
him. Even his friends, the faithful hawks, left him. According to the story, he and all his descendants must
suffer from the curse until the last one dies."

To an eleven-year-old boy with a well-developed sense
of imagination this sounded like grist for my poetic mill.
Had I not seen the actual publication of my first slender
volume of poems (paid for by my uncle Henry) only the
winter before? The Habsburg saga was the stuff mysterious adventure stories are made of.

However, I forgot all about the incident until forty
years later. Again I was approaching the hill upon which
the Habsburg stands. Only this time I had come on purpose to check out the legendary Habsburg curse with the
help of a renowned German psychic, Arthur Orlop,
whom I had imported all the way from Mannheim to as-
sist me in my quest.

A few months before my visit the dimming memory of
the Habsburg curse had been brought back to my attention while I was reading some popular magazines that
dealt somewhat superficially with astrology, the occult
and parapsychology. In the magazine *Prediction* I saw a
two-paragraph mention of the ancient Habsburg curse.
The story was simple enough: A reader was advising the

editors of the existence of an authentic curse concerning the Habsburg family and castle. In essence, it was Monsieur Koehler's story except that in this version the hawks would leave when it was all over and done with. So long as a single hawk remained faithful to the Habsburg, the curse had not found its mark fully. But the story did not elaborate the reasons for the curse nor did it give the name of the one who caused it.

Under the circumstances, I wondered how much was true and how much fictional about the old legend. I discovered that doing research about curses is no way to endear yourself to the head of major libraries or research centers. Finally, however, I remembered a young history teacher I had known many years before when I lived in Vienna. His peculiar specialty had been the collecting of folkloric material and attempting to corroborate it whenever possible.

Dr. J. K. was no longer young when I got him on the telephone in Vienna, but he was glad to talk to me. I met him in a little cafe near his old home.

"The Habsburg curse?" he said as soon as I had stated my purpose. "Oh, I've heard of it, of course—years and years ago. Something about a young man who violates a girl."

My ears perked up. Some new material was being added to the story. I urged Dr. K. to search the deepest recesses of his memory and tell me what he knew, whether or not he could "prove" it in the records.

Dr. K. was sure the legend had started during the second half of the twelfth century when the Habsburg Castle was fairly new and the family, lately come from Alsace, was beginning to feel its oats. The way Dr. K. heard it when he traveled in Switzerland as a young teacher, the

Habsburg curse started with one of the counts who became attracted to a beauty in the village below the hill.

In the abrupt manner of the times, a love affair followed, or perhaps he raped her, or perhaps a little bit of
both. In time, the girl became pregnant. This was the
more deplorable as she had been engaged to be married
to a nice young man in the village before the roving eye
of the count had fallen upon her. The village swain
wanted nothing further to do with her, of course, since it
seems this was still before the age of chivalry. Disowned
also by her own family, she had no place to go but up to
the castle to confront her seducer.

The story is somewhat vague on this point. According
to Dr. K., one source at the Zurich City Museum told him
the count had given orders to keep her out of the castle,
but she sneaked in the back way. The other version,
heard by Dr. K. from people in the vicinity when he last
visited there in the 1930s, had the count *invite* her to his
lair in order to do her in.

Either way, the count wanted nothing to do with her.
She probably became hysterical, and he had her thrown
into the dungeon.

At this point, Dr. K. thinks the distraught girl may have
uttered a curse against Count Habsburg and his family,
taking the hawks in the yard as her witnesses. As long as
there is a Habsburg left alive, there will be birds around
the castle, but when the curse has finally found its mark,
the birds will leave as a sign that it is all over.

(The idea that birds cannot exist in an atmosphere of
death is not new. Dark-colored or black birds are considered bearers of ill fortune or destiny in many civiliza-
tions. During eclipses birds sometimes cannot sing or
move about freely. In an atmosphere heavily laden with

guilt and fear, the highly attuned birds may indeed find themselves disturbed and leave. It has been shown that birds have strong psychic sensitivity, and it may be that there is some truth to this occult imagery.)

The story goes on to say that the girl died in childbirth and was buried with her baby on the grounds.

"There is something in the old Muri chronicle hinting at this kind of trouble," Dr. K. explained to me as he sipped his *Schale Gold*, his light Viennese coffee. "But we can't be too sure since neither the count nor the girl is mentioned by name. But there is a second legend, also of Aargau origin, told around that area. It may well connect."

I did not interrupt, and after a moment my old history teacher continued.

"One of the young counts was killed in a hunting accident. An arrow meant for a stag hit him instead. The next day his body was brought back from the woods and the commotion allegedly aroused the villagers to run out of their houses and see what had happened. The mother of a girl who had been wronged by one of the men at the castle was among those who ran to look, but as she opened her door she almost fell over the body of a large bird. It was a hawk lying dead at her doorstep."

"Sounds like a nice medieval fairy tale to me," I could not help saying.

"It does indeed," Dr. K. agreed. "But it may just be the same girl and the same man. Who knows?"

I asked Dr. K. to try and dig up some additional material on this legend and on the curse and to send it to me in New York. Before he had a chance to do anything about it, however, Dr. K. passed on, leaving to his heirs a fascinating, if very illegible, stack of notes and research papers.

Where exactly did the Habsburgs come from? It appears certain that the ancestors were the dukes of Suevia and Alsace of the Eticho family. One of the most reliable documents on this early period in the history of the Habsburg family are the so-called annals of Muri, a monastery founded by the Habsburgs. Written in the twelfth century, these annals were only discovered in the 1600s. They contain much of the early chronicle of western Switzerland, especially as it pertains to the Habsburgs who lived in the area. From these annals, we learn that a certain Count Guntram, who ruled the northern territory of Alsace, got into some trouble with his Emperor, Otto I, in the year 952. Whatever the cause of the argument, the Emperor declared him disloyal and Count Guntram lost most of his possessions, although, apparently, he somehow managed to get back into the Emperor's graces at a later date, for the northern territories can be traced among the Habsburg family possessions. (Incidentally, Guntram was known as Guntram the Rich, so whatever lands he lost must have been considerable.) Among the territories he apparently did not have to give up when he was in disfavor with the Emperor was a considerable piece of land in western Switzerland near the merger of the rivers Aare and Reuss. This is in the present Swiss canton Aargau, about an hour-and-a-half drive by car from Zurich, and contains mainly rich fertile soil particularly suitable for agriculture, which is still being practiced there today. The piece of land close to the point to where the two rivers meet is called the Eigen.

In addition to his Swiss possessions, Guntram also had considerable land in today's Alsace-Lorraine. The entire area is situated at a crossroads of cultural and political conflict between western and central Europe and has remained important from the beginning of recorded history.

Guntram's son, Lanzelin, increased his father's holdings and the next in line, a certain Radbot, was already a major power in the area. In 1020 Radbot felt himself powerful enough to become the founder of the Benedictine Abbey Muri and of a nunnery nearby at Hermetswyl. It is at Muri that the Habsburg family chronicle has been deposited ever since.

Things were going well for the heirs of Count Guntram. As yet there was no distinctive family name, but Lanzelin was referred to as Count of the Northern Territories and sometimes also as Count of Altenberg, although the latter designation does not seem to be borne out by historical records and thus is legendary rather than documented. It is easy to see why the contemporaries did not care to refer to this family in any particular way since their reputation was then an ambiguous one. On one hand, the counts of the northern territories owned a great deal of land on both sides of the Rhine and were considered wealthy indeed. On the other hand, they still had the reputation of being traitors to the Emperor, and this memory lingered on for quite a while despite the fact that the family later got back into good graces with the Imperial throne.

But the family couldn't care less. They were busy accumulating properties and marrying well. Radbot managed to bring home Ita, the daughter of the Duke of Lorraine, while his brother Rudolph became the husband of Kunigund, daughter of the illustrious House of Zollern, the ancestral family of the Prussian royal house. The third son, also named Lanzelin, managed to marry the daughter of the wealthy Count Von Villingen, a family that later became powerful in southern Germany and northern Switzerland and for centuries owned the area around the present Swiss capital, Zurich. All in all, Lanzelin's sons did very well indeed, although Count Radbot had done best by marrying Princess Ita of Lorraine. Her brother, Bishop Werner of Strasbourg, was then a powerful political figure and couldn't help but increase the prestige and the holdings of his new brother-in-law.

With so many scattered territories on both sides of the Rhine, it became apparent that some sort of focal point was necessary, and shortly after 1020 Count Radbot decided to build himself a new castle. He picked for a site the flat area at the confluence of the rivers Reuss and Aare because it was here that the very center of his possessions was. Then, too, the position was one of geographical advantage. In this flat area there rose a small hill whence one could defend the surrounding countryside easily and with comparatively few soldiers. Upon this hill he built himself his castle. The castle has the appearance and shape of a large square tower with a palas or courtyard on one side. Rising to four stories, it affords a majestic view especially when seen from about a half a mile away in the plains.

However, it lacked a surrounding wall which in those days was generally supported by small turrets the better to defend it against hostile marauders. There is a legend said to explain the absence of a surrounding wall.

Shortly after Count Radbot had finished building his castle, he invited his brother-in-law, Werner of Strasbourg, to have a look at it. When the Bishop saw how Radbot had built a castle without walls, he reprimanded him for his thoughtlessness. In reply, the count allegedly promised to build a wall overnight around his castle, the likes of which the Bishop had never seen. When his guest awoke the next morning, Radbot took him to the window and pointed to the "wall" below. There, surrounding the castle, was his entire garrison deployed like a living wall with horsemen standing at regular intervals in the manner of turrets. Bishop Werner shook his head and smiled. He could only commend his brother-in-law for such trust. Truly, he said, the loyalty of his men was his best defense.

At the time when Count Radbot had selected the land on which to build his new castle—the first such castle his family had ever owned—he had become aware of the rather large number of hawks in the area. Falcons, of course, were used in hunting in the Middle Ages, but their common cousin, the hawk, was another kind of bird. Living primarily on small field animals, hawks would congregate around human habitations in the hope of catching mice and other small fur-bearing animals or perhaps finding some of the refuse from the kitchen. Thus, it was not unusual to see hawks in the immediate area of a castle or large house in those days.

It so happened that the new fortress built by Count Radbot was the largest in the area. Not only did the people of northwestern Switzerland realize this, but apparently word had gotten around to the hawks as well. Whatever the reason, from the beginning, the hill upon which the new castle stood had an unusually large contingent of hawks.

The Count took this as a good omen. True, they were not as glamorous as eagles, always considered symbols of royalty or at least extreme nobility, but the mighty hawk was not an animal to be sneezed at, for he was a good hunter and certainly a fierce defender of his own. Thus, the hawk was just as suitable for the symbolic representa-

tive of family honor as the more elevated eagle. Whether
by accident or by design, the fortress soon became known
as the Hawk Castle, in old German, *havichsburg*. The
popular name of the castle pleased the Counts so much
that eventually they decided to assume it officially. Just
when the name Count of Habsburg came officially into
being is not clear, but there is a document dated September 29, 1108, in which Count Otto, the grandson of
Radbot, is designated as *Count of Habsburg*.

II   On the Trail of an Ancient Curse

In an earlier book, *Window to the Past*, I have successfully demonstrated how a psychic person can delve into the imprint left behind by some emotionally tinged past event and reconstruct it or relive it with such clarity and, frequently, in such detail that one can follow up on this material and corroborate it through the usual historical records. Just as Sybil Leek was able to pinpoint the location of the true Camelot in England or the Landfall of the Viking ships on Cape Cod, so I began to wonder whether perhaps I might not go to the Habsburg, to the original castle, and trace the ancient curse. To begin with, I wanted proof that there really was some sort of curse and that the legend and the local traditions were not merely the figment of some storyteller's imagination. I thought that there was a good way of checking up on the veracity of the curse if I brought a sensitive to the castle who would be totally unfamiliar with the curse as well as the castle itself. I, myself, had not read up on the Habsburgs at that point, and other than the general knowledge that a curse existed, I had no knowledge of its details or the nature of the story connected with the curse.

Strange as it may seem, the Habsburg Castle is not a
major tourist attraction now. It may be after this book
appears, but at that time it took some effort to find the
exact location of the ancient building even when speaking to the representatives of Swissair. Finally, with the
help of the Swiss Center in New York City and Zurich, I
managed to get precise routing to the castle and to two
other equally obscure locations in Switzerland. All three
locations, of course, are known to Swiss historians and
probably have meaning for all Swiss children, but to an
average American they mean nothing. I decided to invite
the German psychic Arthur Orlop of Mannheim to meet
me in Zurich and accompany me to three selected locations. Mr. Orlop and I had met previously. He is a reputa-
ble psychic working with doctors on certain aspects of
psychic healing. Also, he has done work in connection
with court cases tracing missing persons and is generally
active as a professional sensitive. Mr. Orlop readily
agreed to come to Switzerland at my request. Naturally, I
did not inform him of the nature of our quest, nor did I
indicate anything beyond the date and meeting point.
The Swiss tourist office kindly put a car and driver at my
disposal. The driver turned out to be an off-duty tourist
executive, a young man by the name of Mario Hefner.
According to my instructions sent ahead, Mr. Hefner was
not to mention the subject of our quest or in any way indicate in conversation during the ride where we might be
at any given time. I did not go so far as to curtain the
windows of the car, but I made every attempt not to let
Mr. Orlop know where we were going to or what town
we might be passing through at any given moment. As
with any good professional medium, Mr. Orlop made no

attempt to question me about this nor did he display any undue curiosity as to where we were or where we had just been. He was far too busy trying to project himself ahead of time to the locations he was going to visit and to try and give me an advance view of what he perceived psychically.

Shortly after we met at the Zurich airport, Mr. Hefner drove us to the outskirts of Zurich and then made for open country. Our first target on this very long day in Switzerland was the Habsburg Castle. We drove past a number of small towns until we arrived at the provincial city of Brugg. During the ride, Mr. Orlop spoke almost incessantly of his past triumphs, something he has in common with almost all successful mediums. But at no time did the conversation get involved with the matter at hand.

A short time after we had left the environs of Brugg, Mr. Orlop handed me three drawings he had done several days before. Two of them, as I discovered later, were connected with other places we were to visit. The third one was germane to our visit to Habsburg Castle. In his artistic and somewhat confused hand, Mr. Orlop had drawn a crude map of the area showing a castle with a broad tower and a somewhat lower main building. Farther down in the drawing was a small river and to the right he had carefully drawn in the main roads. The rest of the drawing was filled with indications of trees, fields, railroad stations and so forth. In his somewhat precise way, he had dated the drawing August 23, 1971, and signed it A. O. In less than an hour I was able to satisfy myself that it was not only accurate in general terms but

even in specific ways such as the appearance of the castle
from the road, the position of roads and river and even
the trees which Mr. Orlop had sketched in were there.

We were now approaching the target area. Looking out
the window, I saw a small road sign reading *"Zur Habsburg"* and I quickly drew my companion's attention in
the opposite direction. That, to the best of my recollection, was the only time the word "Habsburg" appeared
on signs. We turned into a side road and followed a
gently ascending country lane until, at a bend in the road,
there appeared before us the hill crowned by the ancient
Habsburg Castle.

"That's where we are going," Orlop stated.

That, of course, was not a psychic statement. Quite
obviously, there was no other place to go and our car was
slowing down. But in the context of his prior drawing it
had a certain evidential value for me.

At the foot of the hill, Mr. Hefner hesitated driving on
to the castle itself, but in view of the heavy camera equipment I was carrying, I insisted until he managed to drive
all the way to the gate. The ancient Habsburg had recently been turned into a kind of restaurant, and lately
it had become a favorite off-beat place for business meetings and fraternal affairs from nearby Brugg. There were
wooden benches in front of the gate and some workmen
were visible inside the gate trying to repair damaged
areas of the keep.

As is my usual practice when I bring a psychic to an
investigation site, I left Mr. Orlop to roam around freely.
While I was setting up my motion picture camera and
tape recording equipment, he had a chance to sniff out

whatever vibrations of the past might hang on to the old masonry.

What is left today of the old Habsburg Castle is only part of the original building, while later additions have fallen into disrepair and been dismantled. When the finger of fate had called the Habsburgs to bigger and better things in Austria, the castle had gradually lost its brilliance and importance. Eventually, it was turned over to two families of Habsburg administrators, one taking the front part, and the other taking the rear. At the height of its glory towards the end of the thirteenth century, just prior to a Habsburg becoming a German king, the castle was indeed an imposing double structure that boasted many turrets and large rooms. It even had something that is still preserved and is a rarity in medieval castles—an inside toilet. After the glorious time under the founders, the castle fell on hard times. By fourteen hundred the two families of administrators died out, and it was sold to a family named Von Wohlen. Unfortunately, the Von Wohlens soon found themselves the victims of a war between the Republic of Bern and the German Emperor, with the result that they had to submit to the Bernese government, which took over the castle completely in 1457. Five years later, the Bernese sold the castle again, possibly because the repair bills and the upkeep were too much for the thrifty Swiss, although this is pure speculation. The new owner, a certain Hans Arnold Segesser, wasn't particularly happy with it, either. He, in turn, sold the castle to the sisters of nearby Koenigsfelden. But the good sisters evidently did not enjoy their property, either, and let it fall into greater disrepair than ever until finally, in 1490, the government of Bern told them they had better take care of their property or else. (Even though they

had sold the castle, the Bernese republic considered itself
the feudal overlord much in the manner the German
Emperor was the lord of his noble vassals.) The Bernese
reminded the sisters that the castle was, after all, of
great historical importance and had been entrusted to
them, the Bernese government. Later, the abbey was dis-
solved and Bern took back full possession of the Habsburg.

By 1553 the castle was in such a state of disrepair the
Bernese government decided to save what could be
saved. The original invoices of all those efforts are still
preserved, and it appears that the Bernese did indeed
spend a good deal of money to save the Habsburg from
total ruin. It was in vain, however, for by the eighteenth
century, the Habsburg was nothing but a ruin inhabited
by itinerant farmers and neglected even by the Bernese
government. The Bernese might have had to spend even
more money to restore the ancient ruin had not the
Napoleonic Wars redistributed some of the Swiss land.

In 1804 the Habsburg and the land around it was
handed over to the neighboring canton of Aargau, and
the Bernese could finally wash their hands of it.

Since then, minor restorations have continued—the last
ones in 1949. What remains now is pretty much the oldest part of the castle while the second half has long been
removed, or rather what was left of it by the nineteenth
century. Nevertheless, the remaining exterior is still imposing as it gazes out from its castle hill over the Swiss
landscape with the Rhine in the distance and France and
Germany beyond.

We entered the castle through a Gothic arch, walked
up wooden stairs that were so new workmen were still
finishing them. In the upper stories some of the ancient

rooms were being restored to their original shape. A year
or two from now the Habsburg might indeed be an imposing tourist attraction.

After I had inspected the upper three stories, I noticed
a door leading to the cellar. It was locked. I summoned
the lady who ran the restaurant and asked to go down
into the cellar. She shook her head. That was not possible, she said. Down there was private property. Mr. Hefner explained who I was and why I had come all the way
from America and that I was not about to be barred by
such a minor matter as the cellar being private property
when, quite obviously, there might be something terribly
important down there. After a moment's hesitation, the
lady brought the key and unlocked the door. We walked
down a musty flight of stairs into what was once the
Habsburg cellar. Now I understood why it was off limits
to casual visitors. It was filled with bottles of wine and
other supplies for the restaurant.

Mr. Orlop was not impressed by that, however, as he
scurried about pointing out "hot spots" of a psychic nature to me so that I might take photographs of them. As
a matter of fact, when it was developed, one of the photographs showed whitish emanations in the area of the
stairs.

As we had neared the castle earlier, Mr. Orlop had
made a cryptic remark that led me to believe he was already on to some sort of story connected with the castle.

"There is a girl involved, a young girl, and there is an
illegitimate child, too," he had mumbled.

Now I faced the medium in the heart of Habsburg
Castle.

"Tell me, Mr. Orlop. Do you know where we are?"

"I haven't the slightest idea."

"What is your impression of this building?"

"I think this castle has some historical significance, but there is something else of importance apart from its historical connotations," he replied.

"Tell me about the past of this building."

"This castle was built by a man who came from far away," Mr. Orlop said. "I get the feeling of two brothers and their families. One, the taller one, brought about some innovations in the area. Their descendants still live. Descendants of this family went elsewhere, even across the water."

"Can you get any names?" I urged.

Mr. Orlop thought this over for a moment and then looked at me with a puzzled expression on his face.

"I get a name like *vulture*," he said. "I don't understand it. What has a vulture got to do with this family?"

"What about this vulture family?" I inquired. I realized immediately that the medium was getting his birds confused. What he saw psychically looked to him like a vulture. To someone else it might very well suggest a hawk. The hawks of the Habsburgs perhaps. Quite obviously, the name of this ancient family that was connected with the castle had something to do with a large bird of prey. That in itself I thought was evidential enough to pursue this line of questioning further.

"What kind of people were these vulture people?" I asked.

Orlop shrugged.

"Well, they quarreled a lot among themselves," he replied. "One of the vulture brothers built something else down in the valley."

To Mr. Orlop it looked like a large building and suggested a kind of factory. Could he have been referring to the Abbey of Muri founded about the same time as the castle itself?

"Do you have any impression of evil or negative events connected with this building?"

Orlop nodded emphatically.

"Yes, indeed, I do. It goes back to a young girl. It had to do with an illegitimate child and involved the tall one of the vulture brothers. All this happened a long time ago."

I decided to test Mr. Orlop directly.

"Is there any sort of curse attached to this building?"

What emerged now was a story of the kind that could have happened at any time but particularly in the Middle Ages where class distinctions were still deep and serfdom was part and parcel of the economic life. It appears, according to Mr. Orlop, that a curse was uttered by a woman who had become pregnant by the lord of the manor. The girl was scheduled to marry a prominent citizen in her own village, but her husband-to-be refused to marry her because of the affair. In anger, Mr. Orlop explained, the girl cursed her own child and its father for all time to come.

"What happened to the child?" I asked.

"The child was removed. It was killed and is buried somewhere here on the castle grounds."

In addition it appears the girl had also cursed the man in the village who had refused to marry her.

"What happened to the curse? Did it continue?"

"The curse continued even though many members of the vulture family did not believe in it. It shows itself not only economically but through certain diseases."

"What did the descendants of the vulture family do in later centuries?"

"One member of the family, a tall man, was responsible for some important reforms, setting things right."

During our inspection of the castle, Mr. Orlop suddenly rushed outside the walls to a spot on the grounds where there was a heavy iron trap door. The lid was too heavy for me to move, but as I walked away to get help, Mr. Orlop, as though supported by unseen forces, managed to move it easily and quickly. He peered down into the dark recess, shook his head, but said nothing. After carefully closing the lid again, he joined me in further exploration of the castle. I asked him what exactly he had felt to be under the lid outside the wall.

"I thought it was a well used to throw people in, people that were worrisome to the owners of the castle. In particular, I sensed a woman, and there is a man, too, someone connected with the castle itself."

"But who are those two?"

"Those two early members of the vulture family, the man and the girl with the illegitimate child. They were down there."

There was nothing more, and it seemed as if Mr. Orlop had exhausted his supply of psychic information. We had some lunch and shortly afterward rode down the hill towards eastern Switzerland on the second leg of our expedition tracing the beginnings of the Habsburgs and, of course, the Habsburg curse.

Although I did not realize it at the time of my visit, the physical description given by the medium of the great man among the early owners of the castle fitted pretty well the physical description of Rudolph I, the very first Habsburg to wear the German crown. He had resided at the castle, but had left when the call to rule Germany came. I had not expected to find the imprints of the more famous Habsburg princes in this castle since the family had really never come back after they had become prominent in Germany and Austria. But the memory of it somehow clung to the walls of the ancient fortress. How else could Mr. Orlop have spoken of the "vultures" and the vulture castle? I could not help but wonder who the practical joker was who supplied the medium with his information—changing hawks to vultures in a fine display of political satire, for truly, if anything fitted the Habsburgs in those early days, it was the name "vulture," not "hawk."

III The Curse Begins to Work

On examining the historical evidence, we must not jump
to the conclusion that every unfortunate event, every
death, every political failure was due to a curse. With an
ambitious family like the Habsburgs, a number of successes and a number of failures are natural. It is only
when the negative events take on *a certain pattern,* a certain repetition, or when the losses hint at the unexpected
that we must take into consideration the possibility of a
curse.

The House of Habsburgs, or, as it was later called, the
House of Austria, certainly had many periods of great
success. There is no denying that the Habsburgs frequently gained their objectives in world history, but curiously enough, in most cases, just after gaining some
high plateau of success there came an unexpected, sudden reverse, as if the family was never to be left in a
position to enjoy their triumphs for very long.

The first time we can say with any degree of certainty
that the curse became operative was in the life of Count
Albert, the fourth Habsburg to bear this name. Albert
entered the scene at a time when the family was marrying
well and wisely—not for love, of course, but for real

estate. His wife was Heilwic von Kyburg, one of the wealthiest heiresses around. From that marriage came roughly one third of the later Habsburg real estate, for the families the Habsburgs married into somehow died out pretty quickly, leaving their estates to them. Albert did well on his own, too. Since he was the eldest son, when his father died in 1232, Albert inherited the major share of his possessions. These possessions included large parts of Alsace, the administration of Murbach, part of what is today the canton Zurich, and, of course, the Habsburg home grounds in Aargau with the proud castle. His younger brother founded a sideline of the house on much more modest territories near Zurich.

Thus, Albert ruled over a considerable stretch of land in northwestern Switzerland. His reputation was that of a fair prince and his family life was above reproach. Contemporary sources speak of the Countess Heilwic as being exceptionally "fair," meaning beautiful. Fate had given the young couple a son whom they called Rudolph after the count's father. This boy was to become the illustrious Rudolph von Habsburg, who emerged from the German Interregnum—the civil wars—as the first German Emperor of the House of Habsburg.

In his early twenties when he came to rule, Albert was on top of his world, so it seemed only right that he accept an Imperial invitation to join the many other knights who were planning another crusade to liberate the Holy Land.

This crusade, the fifth, was more successful than some of the others undertaken by the Christian rulers of Europe, who, under Papal urging, acted in the mistaken belief that Palestine had to be liberated from the benighted Moslems. In a hard and fast campaign from 1228 to 1229, the Christians managed to force the Sultan El-

Kamil to surrender Jerusalem and sign a peace treaty
with them. The Holy Roman Emperor Frederick II himself
came to Jerusalem to be crowned, an occasion of such
mystical significance that thereafter all Holy Roman and
German Emperors considered themselves "King of Jerusalem," whether or not they had ever been there.

From 1229 to 1239 the Holy Land again was a quasi-
European feudal kingdom where the crusaders lived off
the land and enjoyed themselves immensely since there
was very little warfare. But matters got worse eventually
as the Egyptian army became restless. During one of the
many "unofficial" border battles with raiding Arabs,
Count Albert von Habsburg and his small band of knights
were wiped out. Four years later Jerusalem fell to an
army of Asiatic mercenaries in the service of the Egyptian
Sultan.

The irony of it was that Count Albert had survived
the major battles and was about to return home, when a
routine patrol took his life. Still in his twenties, he had
ruled over his lands a mere seven years.

Even during Albert's short reign there had been difficulty with his relatives concerning the division of properties. A temporary arrangement had split the Habsburgs
into two houses, but the solution was not a happy one.
Albert and his brother Rudolph finally invoked arbitra-
tion, but it failed to settle anything, for the two houses
went to war against each other as part of the greater
conflict between Pope and Emperor, and as a result,
much was lost. Only years later did the two Habsburg
lines become reconciled with each other again.

When Albert IV was killed he left a capable son who
was to play an important role in history. Rudolph looked
the mighty ruler. Tall, slim and possessed of a pale intel-

lectual face, he was a soft-spoken man given to moderation and, as a contemporary chronicle reports, "Since his
early youth, warlike but clever and favored by fate, a tall
man with a hooked nose, serious expression, whose dig-
nity and strength of character was borne out by his appearance."

Rudolph's elevation to the highest office in the land
came about simply because he was then considered one
of the least powerful noblemen capable of administering
the large German Empire. The electors, that is to say, the
princes who had the power to select a new Emperor,
would not trust one of their own number to become King
of Germany. The Pope, whose job it was to crown the
German King and thus make him Emperor, was not likely
to support a powerful individual in that post. The long
conflict between the German Emperors of the House of
Staufen and the Popes had ended with the excommunica-
tion and finally the death of the last Staufen Emperor.
During the intervening years disorder had been the pre-
dominant factor in Europe, especially in Germany. Although the princes and the Pope wanted order to be
restored, they did not wish to have the power concen-
trated once again in the hands of a powerful family such
as the Staufens. When they had exhausted just about all
the possibilities of a candidate, they came upon the name
of Rudolph von Habsburg, a minor, capable and otherwise uncommitted count in northwestern Switzerland
and Alsace. A deputation was dispatched and the German crown offered Rudolph, who accepted immediately.

To everyone's surprise, however, the count turned out
to be more than a humble administrator willing to do
what the princes and the Pope told him to do. As time
went on he showed his mettle. This shrewd man wanted
above all to be on good terms with both the German

princes and the Pope. To make the Pope aware of his religious inclinations, he made sure that an incident early
in his career was reported back to Rome. It seems that
Rudolph was about to cross a river in Switzerland when a
priest came along on his way to a dying man. The priest
was carrying the sacrament but had no way of getting
across the river. With no hesitation, Rudolph offered
him his horse. After the priest had crossed the river, Rudolph gave him the steed with the remark that any horse
that had carried the sacrament would no longer be suitable for ordinary usage or warlike purposes.

During his coronation, it developed that the Imperial
scepter was missing, but this was not surprising since there
had been civil disorders for many years previously, and
many things had been mislaid or lost. In the embarrass-
ment of the moment, Rudolph proved himself equal to
the situation. With a flourish, he seized the crucifix from
the high altar, lifted it up and declared, "Here is the
symbol that has delivered us and the entire world. Let it
be my scepter on this occasion." With that he proceeded
to confirm the rights of each individual German prince,
using the crucifix as his scepter. Contemporary witnesses
reported seeing a reddish cloud above the cathedral at
Aix-la-Chapelle during the coronation ceremony. The
cloud took on the shape of a cross, which led the witnesses to assume that Rudolph von Habsburg was indeed
the true successor to the first Christian Emperor, the
Roman Constantine. But the cross which the Habsburgs
were yet to bear in the ensuing centuries might also be
seen in the seemingly supernatural appearance of a cruci-
form cloud.

Rudolph's election to the highest position in the land
came as a bitter disappointment to Ottocar, King of Bohemia, who had himself coveted the crown of Germany.

As a result, war between the two kings was inevitable.
Two campaigns were fought and in the end, Ottocar lost
both his land and his life. The "impoverished Swiss
count," as his enemies used to call Rudolph, was now a
major political figure in Europe. In August 1278 Rudolph
stood at the zenith of his power and immediately set
about to cement his dynasty's hold on the hereditary
lands of Austria, Styria and Carinthia as well as the Swiss
and southern German possessions. Fortunately, he had
six daughters and since political marriages were the only
way the ruling class saw unions between men and
women in their families, Rudolph did what he could
to use his natural capital, as he considered his daughters,
to the advantage of the family, regardless of individual
desires of the young women. He even managed to reach
out towards England by planning the marriage of his son
Hartmann with the royal Princess Joan.

Everything seemed just great, but suddenly, one by
one, fate took away all his pleasures. Although he was
getting along in years, his wife bore him two more children, both of whom died of unknown causes while still
infants. Shortly after their deaths, his wife Anna passed
away. Then a few days before Christmas of the same
year, 1281, his son Hartmann drowned at age eighteen.
The accident was particularly tragic. Hartmann was
crossing the river Rhine from Breisach to Oppenheim,
where his father was waiting for him, when his small boat
was seized by the strong current and turned over. Pulled
down by his heavy armor, the young man was unable to
escape and drowned in the icy waters of the Rhine. With
him went Rudolph's hopes of drawing England into the
Habsburg sphere of interest.

One of the peculiarities of the Habsburg family is the
inheritance "to joint hands." This means that all proper-

ties belong to all male members of the family and are administered jointly. In theory, this may work out fine and avoid injustices, but in practice it has led to many misunderstandings and even to intrafamily wars and dissension. Why the Habsburgs used this rare and difficult principle of inheritance is not clear. The majority of other noble families had, by the thirteenth century, recognized the advantages of the right of the first born and thus avoided splitting off properties and weakening family power.

Since the King felt that his days were numbered, he arranged for his sons, Albert and Rudolph, to become administrators of the Austrian lands. However, following in the tradition of his house Rudolph appointed his sons together rather than separately. This did not sit well with the two princes, and they complained about it. Under the circumstances, Rudolph changed his decision a year later and decided that Albert should rule alone in Austria and that Rudolph would be taken care of in other ways. Unfortunately, the younger Rudolph wasn't taken care of to his satisfaction, and as a result, his heirs later took matters into their own hands.

In his declining years the Emperor knew nothing but misery. For one thing he was unable to secure the German crown for his son Albert. The German princes refused to recognize Albert's right until his father had been crowned by the Pope in Rome. Because of his health and dynastic pride, however, Rudolph could not undertake the long and perilous journey, thereby giving the German princes an excuse to by-pass Albert. Then, too, the more territory he acquired in the Swiss area, the more the people of that area turned against the Habsburgs. The beginnings of the Swiss Federation were already being felt, and the people of northwestern Switzerland were

biding their time until they could proceed against the
two powerful overlords.

But what appeared as a natural chain of events, the
election of his son as Heir Presumptive, was denied Rudolph and he died uncertain as to the fate of his family,
uncertain as to the future of the very Empire he had
helped resurrect from its ashes. In contemplating his long
reign, Rudolph is said to have remarked wryly that he
had always believed in a policy of the possible, but that
sometimes the possible was impossible.

Albert succeeded his father in the Austrian territories
and in Switzerland and southwestern Germany, but the
royal or, even more, the Imperial crown was yet to be
won. Only many years later did Albert succeed in win-
ning the German crown. At the time, he had to accept
the bitter news of another man's election to the high office, even though in his heart he felt it an injustice. Almost meekly, he turned over the Imperial insignia to
Adolph of Nassau while at the same time planning to
fortify and enlarge his position in Austria and the eastern
territories.

Three years after his father's death, Albert suffered
what he at first thought was a "strange malady." The fact
of the matter was he had been poisoned during one of
the rounds of state dinners that were the medieval way
of making friends or disarming potential enemies. Because of this custom, in the first years of his reign, Albert
traveled about quite a bit, eating and drinking with many
of his "friends" and potential rivals for the German territories his father had wanted, but not succeeded in
acquiring.

Rumor had it that the Bohemian King Wenceslas, Albert's brother-in-law, was behind the poisoning, revenge

for the defeat his father, King Ottocar, had suffered at the hands of the Emperor Rudolph.

Whatever the reason, it soon became clear that Albert had a vicious poison in his body and something had to be done about it before it killed him. The physicians in 1295, of course, did not know as much about illness and its cures as we know today, and their methods were often crude and more damaging than useful.

A council of medical practitioners was called and it was decided to "drain" the poison out of Albert's system. This was to be accomplished by the ingenious method of hanging the poor man by his feet for long periods of time to give the poison a chance to "drain" off. After several days of this inhuman treatment, Albert lost consciousness, and the pressure from the blood rushing to his head destroyed the sight in one eye. Now he not only was weak from the effects of the poison, but also half-blind.

Far from handsome to begin with, this added misfortune turned Albert into an evil-looking monster at the sight of whom women would turn away and even hardened soldiers shuddered.

In the middle ages, it was believed that anyone "struck" by the misfortune of an ugly face or damage to his body had somehow offended God and was being punished for his sins. Thus, the insidious result of Albert's appearance was the belief that the Habsburg prince had been struck down by fate.

Albert's tragedy, together with the inevitable uncertainty after a major change of government, gave the Swiss new hopes of proceeding against their hated oppressor.

As soon as the news reached them of King Rudolph's death in 1291, the people of northwestern Switzerland

had secretly assembled to attempt to regain their ancient
rights and freedoms. In particular, the representatives of
the three forest communities of Uri, Schwyz and Unterwalden came together on a hill called Mount Ruetli to
take an Oath of Mutual Assistance against the Habsburgs.
A few months later this new coalition entered into political treaties with the powerful city of Zurich and other
anti-Habsburg communities in northern Switzerland and
even with Savoy.

The Oath of Mutual Assistance was the beginning of
the end for the Habsburgs in Switzerland. As the German
dramatist Friedrich von Schiller put it in *William Tell,*
"We want to be a united people of brothers not to separate in need or danger." It is in this context and out of
this atmosphere of secret and semi-secret meetings
among the Swiss that the quasi-legendary account of William Tell came into being. The villain of the Tell story,
the Habsburg administrator Herman Gessner, is a historical figure. Swiss spies had supplied William Tell and
his fellow conspirators with the news that Gessner was
to pass through a certain narrow valley called the Hollow
Lane not far from the town of Kuessnach. All Tell had
to do was lie in wait at the valley and pick off the Habsburg official as he passed on his horse. This is precisely
what happened, and the Swiss, knowing the time had
come, rose up against their Habsburg enemies.

Schiller places this chain of events in the last years of
Albert's reign. Within a few months after Gessner's death,
the administrators of the absentee Habsburgs had all they
could do to maintain themselves in their strongpoints.
The open land was uncertain territory, and no Habsburg
knight would venture forth very far alone.

Coupled with this misfortune, Albert also had to deal
with revolt in Austria itself, for the Austrians preferred

the Bohemian King to the rule of the Habsburgs. In 1287 Vienna rose in revolt, but the rebellion was put down with great cruelty by Albert, who had imported large contingents of West German mercenaries to fight for him. This action did not exactly endear him to his Austrian subjects. Four years later the Styrian nobility rose against him, followed by the Austrian native princes in 1295. To make things even more complicated, Albert was engaged in a long-running battle with the Archbishop of Salzburg.

A veritable "chain of disasters" had broken loose over his head. In the past, one or two battles might have been fought simultaneously. But now everybody was up in arms. The Swiss were trying to free themselves, and the Austrians were trying to get home rule and trade rights while playing the Hungarians against him, the Bohemians against the Hungarians, and in general making capital out of his predicament. Albert himself began to believe he was damned, for he connected his physical problems with his political disasters.

Despite his failing faith in himself, Albert managed to survive the pressures around him by giving in—as little as possible, of course, but enough to persuade the various factions in revolt against him to calm down. The shrewd ruler figured he could always break his word later on when he was back in full power. Incidentally, this was a frequent Habsburg trait, although other ruling houses have shown it, too. The Austrian nobility got their privileges under duress, the Styrians were assured Albert respected their importance to his rule, and even the rebellious Swiss were at least kept at bay.

Doubtless, Albert would have managed eventually to calm all the troubled waters around him had it not been for his own greed. It appeared perfectly natural to him to yield territory to a superior enemy when required, or to give in to the hated estates on matters of home rule if thereby he could save his neck for a while. But to consider the rights of relatives without power to enforce them was not within him.

As has been mentioned, Rudolph, Albert's father, had originally divided his possessions between his two sons, Albert and Rudolph, but he later amended this decision by leaving everything to Albert. Now Albert's nephew, John, carried on the feeling that an injustice had been committed against his father, Rudolph, and hence against his side of the house of Habsburg. As he grew to manhood he carried this deep conviction within himself hoping that he might persuade his uncle Albert to part with some of his territories and thus right the ancient wrong.

But Albert was now also the German King. His belated accession to the German throne had been made possible mainly by the dissatisfaction of the German princes with Adolph of Nassau whom they had finally removed in favor of Albert. Thus, the Habsburgs regained the German crown. With so much power in his hands, Albert paid scant attention to the demands made upon him by his nephew. Despite the pleas of John's mother and despite several trips John made to Switzerland to talk to his uncle about the matter, Albert refused to receive him.

Finally, for reasons of courtesy rather than any real desire to see his "dear nephew," Albert invited John to a dinner he was to give at Winterthur. But this was not a private audience in which such delicate matters as ancient wrongs could be discussed. Several other distant cousins of Albert would also be present; it was a family affair rather than a political meeting. A generation back the parents of these cousins had been equals with Albert's father, but now they had to bow low before their royal cousin Albert and obey the ceremonial of the court. Naturally, they resented this. Driven by the burning desire to revenge the wrong done his father, John regaled his cousins with his plight. They, too, had grievances against their more successful cousin but nothing as fundamental as John's claim. However, they reinforced John's belief that he had to take some sort of action to get his share of the rich inheritance. When John left the family dinner he hated his uncle even more. A sense of destiny made him linger on in Switzerland, however, and on May 1, 1308, he felt that his time had come. While King Albert was making preparations to cross the river Reuss near Windisch, John persuaded the Swiss freedom fighters to join him in attacking Albert. Three of the free Swiss joined him that morning, bent on doing what they felt was their patriotic duty. As the King passed by within sight of the Habsburg Castle, they bolted from behind some bushes and knifed him to death.

Suddenly the ancient wrong done John's father was forgotten. Europe spoke only of John, the uncle murderer, John Parricida, the horrible creature who underhandedly had taken the life of a close relative. The sensitivities of medieval society were upset by the deed, even though killings were the order of the day all around Europe. In *William Tell*, Schiller gives us a scene in which John Parricida flees for his life, driven not only by the danger of imminent arrest, but also by the furies of his conscience, though I very much doubt that John felt guilty about what he had done. As it turned out, however, Albert's family took cruel and long-lasting revenge on John's family and friends and many lives were snuffed out because of the murder of King Albert. Not for the first time, and unfortunately not for the last, did an inner

conflict rend the Habsburgs asunder, pitting cousin
against cousin, even brother against brother.

The murder of Albert had immediate consequences in
Germany. The princes were not exactly unhappy over
the sudden removal of a man they had begun to eye
suspiciously as becoming far too powerful for their taste,
so, rather than elect Albert's son and successor, they
turned to another weak individual as they had done twice
before. Thus, they elected Henry of Luxembourg to succeed the murdered king. Once again, the Holy Roman
Crown of Germany was lost to the Habsburgs.

Meanwhile, Albert's sons were busy exterminating the
descendants of the four men who had murdered the
King. This did not endear them to the Swiss who considered the murder a political deed rather than a common crime as claimed by the Habsburg family. Under
the circumstances, an open conflict between the forming
Swiss National Federation and the entrenched Habsburg
interests as represented by the Habsburgs themselves and
their allies in Switzerland seemed inevitable. The clever
Swiss managed to maneuver things in such a way that
they could choose the spot where the encounter would
take place. They had on their side a greater knowledge
of the territory and an inborn fervor to defend their
homes. The Habsburgs and their allies, on the other hand,
had to rely on imported mercenaries and, at the very best,
on the doubtful loyalty of city people and some local
nobility.

While the political situation in Switzerland slowly
came to a boiling point, things did not fare too well for
the Habsburgs in Germany, either. After the death of
Emperor Henry VII, the German princes failed to agree
on a candidate with the result that they elected two Em-

perors. Both Louis of Bavaria and Frederick the Handsome, Albert's son and successor, were elected to the German throne. The double election of 1314 made things even more difficult for the Habsburgs in their original territories in Switzerland and southwestern Germany. The Swiss became partisans of one or the other Imperial Pretender, and as a result, the comparatively small war which loomed in Switzerland took on the overtones of a major battle for Europe itself. When Louis of Bavaria confirmed the ancient privileges of the Swiss cantons, the decision became clear. By and large, the Swiss sided with the Bavarian rather than the Habsburg.

For the third time within a scant twenty years the Habsburgs were being robbed of the German crown. For the third time a seemingly kind fate that had elevated them to a prominent position in Europe with one hand took away with the other what it had previously granted. A sense of frustration permeated the halls of the Habsburgs wherever they resided, whether in Vienna or in Styria or in Switzerland itself.

While all of Europe watched and wondered whether the dark clouds over the House of Habsburg would ever lift again, matters came to a head in a winding valley near the Swiss city of Zug. Dominating this valley along the coast of Lake Aegeri is a steep hill called Mount Morgarten. It was here that a battle of great significance took place on November 15, 1315.

IV An Ominous Defeat and Its Consequences

A short time after Arthur Orlop and I entered the territory of the canton Schwyz, the calm clear waters of Lake Aegeri appeared on our right. To the left and coming close to the road itself was the steep descent of Mount Morgarten. Between the mountain and the lake there was precious little space for anyone to pass, and I realized why this had become a fateful milestone in the history of the Habsburg Empire.

We were actually tracing the journey of that ill-fated army which was surprised by the Swiss freedom fighters back in 1315. Earlier that day we had already been to the ancient Habsburg fortress in the northwest of Switzerland. I carefully studied the second of the three drawings Mr. Orlop had given me and which he had drawn while in an inspired state several days prior to our meeting. The drawing seemed confused to me at first, but on close inspection, I realized that he had somehow foreseen a visit to this very spot. Remarks such as "high underbrush to the right" or "sandy road and steep path" were found to be correct on examination of the territory later on. Mr. Orlop had no idea where we were going or why we were undertaking this particular part of the journey, although

Mario Hefner, the Swiss tourist executive who had vol-
unteered to drive us, knew, of course, where we were
headed. So did I in a general way. But I think that neither Mr. Hefner nor I had any specific knowledge of the
territory itself. Although Mr. Hefner is Swiss, his education did not include the exact military history of the battleground we were about to enter. As for myself, I learned
all that much later. Thus, we were both interested to see
Mr. Orlop become more and more agitated as the car
rounded the last bend of the lake and came to an abrupt
halt at the foot of a steep hill. That hill was crowned by
a monument inscribed "To the heroes of Morgarten."
The landscape leading up to the monument was carefully
sculptured like a park, and there was a small inn beneath
the hill. Other than the inscription on the monument
itself, there was nothing to indicate even the name of the
area. Mr. Orlop's eyesight was certainly not such that he
could make out the inscription atop the monument from
where we were now standing. Suddenly he began to run
up the steep hill as fast as his legs could carry him, and
Mr. Hefner and I had difficulty following him at times as
he moved now here, now there, around the very steep
high meadow.

As is his custom, Mr. Orlop had made some advance
remarks about the investigation that was to follow while
we were still en route to the location. During the ride
he had remarked to me that he felt someone was involved
who lived in a little house by the side of the lake. I had
been surprised since we were in the middle of nowhere at
that particular moment, and there was no indication that
we were even approaching a lake. The generally known
tourist area of Swiss lakes was far distant from where we
were going. Up to the moment when we actually came
face to face with Lake Aegeri, I, myself, had never

heard of it, yet I have been to Switzerland dozens of times in my life.

And now we stood in back of the monument on Mount Morgarten and the lake, reflecting the bright afternoon sun, blinded us as we looked out into the narrow valley below.

"What do you feel in this area, Mr. Orlop?" I asked.

As yet we had not discussed the purpose of our visit or the nature of the area.

"I feel a large crowd has assembled here," he said. "They are waiting for something. They come from the hinterland. They would like to go down but they are being pushed back."

"Why are they here?"

"They are being pursued by an armed force."

"What exactly happened?"

"I get the feeling that some people are being pushed back. They want to cross the lake, but they do not succeed. Instead, they are being pushed around the corner."

"What is the significance of this place?"

"I have the feeling that something very tragic happened here, but at the same time this event had great significance later on. Someone was elevated to high office here as a consequence, almost like being crowned. I think people were decorated here for this. Some of these people were then made overlords of the land. It is a question of uniting and conquering together."

I walked the psychic across the lower part of the steep meadow and pointed out a small house not far away, close to the lake and yet above it. The house seemed very ancient and I wondered whether it was the building Mr. Orlop had clairvoyantly envisioned en route. He nodded emphatically. Yes, that was the house all right.

I was puzzled by his insistence that someone had been crowned in this meadow. Suddenly, he turned and ran up the steep meadow. He was obviously agitated. Carrying my heavy recording equipment and two cameras, I finally managed to catch up with him.

"Tell me what has happened here that upsets you so much?"

Mr. Orlop, a man in his middle years who is far from athletic, was out of breath.

"I don't like this place," he explained, while trying to catch his breath, "but something terrible happened here on this steep meadow. There were people down below, and I get the feeling that something came down on their heads." For a moment the psychic covered his eyes with his hands almost as if he were reliving the past. "There was a lot of blood shed here, right here."

I confirmed that we were standing in the middle of a battleground but told him no more than that. Again he pointed at the old house in the distance.

"That's where they assembled before they planned this thing," he said dramatically. Then he stepped over towards the monument and pointed at the lake below.

"That lake over there, a lot of them were drowned in it. They couldn't get away. They tried but they couldn't."

I felt chilly despite the warm afternoon sun burning down on us. I had not selected this spot without good reason. It was here that the Habsburg curse showed itself once again in its most surprising and devastating manner.

The War of Mount Morgarten had its beginnings in the arrogant demands made by the sons of King Albert upon the free Swiss of Uri, Schwyz and Unterwalden that they acknowledge Frederick the Handsome of Aus-

tria as the true Emperor. The Swiss, however, preferred
Louis the Bavarian, who had confirmed their ancient
rights. Ever since August 1291, the Oath of Mutual Assistance taken by the representatives of Uri, Schwyz and
Unterwalden at Mount Ruetli against their oppressors
had been a thorn in the flesh of the Habsburgs. Now they
saw their chance to suppress the union of Mount Ruetli
once and for all and thus destroy the incipient formation
of a free Switzerland. With two Emperors to choose between, Frederick and Louis, the Swiss were in a particularly volatile situation. The people of the north and east
living in open flatlands and thus much more vulnerable
to enemy attack than the mountaineering people of the
south had no choice but to stay with the Habsburgs and
Duke Frederick. But the people of the heartlands, especially the three original cantons of Uri, Schwyz and
Unterwalden, who had decided to throw in their fate
with the Bavarian, knew they could defend themselves
if need be against superior enemy forces by withdrawing
into their mountains and making good use of the many
lakes and rivers in their lands. As yet the Habsburgs had
no legal reason to proceed against the three cantons. But
that excuse was given them early in 1314 when the people
of Schwyz attacked the monastery of Einsiedeln over
some local dispute. The Bishop of Constance, who administered this monastery, demanded that the Habsburg
government restore its rights, and the Habsburgs re-
sponded immediately, sensing an opening to proceed
against the free Swiss altogether.

Since Duke Frederick was kept busy defending himself against his competition in Germany itself, he depu-
tized his brother, Duke Leopold, to lead an army against
the free Swiss. Leopold started his campaign by cutting
off food supplies from the three inner Swiss cantons. Then

he assembled as many armed contingents as he could
raise from Austria, the Swiss nobility siding with the
Habsburgs, the bishops and from some of the strongpoints and fortresses owned by the Habsburgs.

From this varied force Leopold managed to assemble
a sizable army. But the Swiss had been looking towards
this day of reckoning for a long time. Even though they
were apparently outnumbered many times over, they did
what they could to fortify their position. They even built
a wall on territory taken from the disputed monastery and
surrounded it wherever they could with palisades, turrets and strongpoints.

Finally, matters came to a head in the summer of 1315
when a sea battle occurred on Lake Lucerne. Duke Leopold moved his troops, alleged to have been twenty
thousand men, into the area of Zug. Between Zug and the
territory of Schwyz lay Lake Aegeri that could only be
passed by way of a narrow road along the shore. On the
other side of that road rose steep Mount Morgarten. Duke
Leopold tried to fool the crafty Swiss with a false attack
farther up north. But it is said that the free Swiss were
warned by a friendly neighbor, a local nobleman named
von Huenenberg. Dispatching an arrow across the lines
into the Swiss camp, he managed to send this message:
"Beware at the Morgarten." Whether this actually happened, or is merely legend, the fact remains that the free
Swiss were amply prepared for the Austrian onslaught.
On the night of November 14, 1315, Duke Leopold and
his army marched out of the city of Zug and prepared to
attack early the next morning. The knights on horseback,
followed by most of the foot soldiers moved slowly along
the shore of Lake Aegeri, thus becoming hemmed in on
one side by the lake and on the other by the mountain.
When their advance patrol encountered no sign of the

hostile Swiss, they continued somewhat carelessly along the lake. The free Swiss, lying in wait high up on the side of Mount Morgarten, knew of the Austrian movements. They had prepared themselves with dozens upon dozens of freshly cut trees and heavy stones—anything they could roll down the steep side of the mountain to crush, or at least confuse, the Austrian army.

Early on the morning of November 15 they did precisely that. When the Austrians realized what was happening and saw the Swiss rushing towards them, they tried to escape by the only route they saw, the narrow pass on the south side of the lake. But they never managed to reach the pass. The Swiss cut them off and forced them into the lake where they drowned. What was left of the Austrian troops—and it wasn't much—retreated to Zug.

The victory at Mount Morgarten was a complete debacle for the Austrians, the more surprising as it had not been anticipated or even thought possible. Fifteen hundred horsemen and five hundred foot soldiers were killed. Duke Leopold of Austria himself barely escaped ahead of his pursuers.

The news of this defeat came as a shock to the Habsburg dukes. But for the moment there was nothing that could be done to bring the Swiss into line. The free Swiss, on the other hand, renewed their ancient union shortly afterwards and in renewing their pledge to elect Louis of Bavaria, they received, in turn, another pledge of their freedom from Habsburg rule.

The insidious aspects of the Habsburg curse became more pronounced as time went on. It seems as though it operated frequently in a way that made it an unpleasant

surprise when it occurred. In the case of the War of
Mount Morgarten, the Habsburgs had every expectation
of victory: overwhelming forces, excellent organization,
an experienced general at the head of the troops, and
the help of native nobles familiar with the territory.
Nevertheless, a tiny band of free Swiss managed to destroy the proud Austrian army in a matter of a few hours.
No wonder, then, that some Europeans wondered
whether the Habsburgs might not be accursed, even at
that early stage.

Arthur Orlop had spoken of this battle as if he had
witnessed it himself. He had accurately pinpointed the
spot where the encounter had taken place, the corner
where the enemy was pushed off into the lake, and it
seemed that perhaps the old house where he felt people
had assembled may have been the spot where the Swiss
had assembled the night before the momentous battle.
Certainly, many brave heroes of this day were decorated
for their bravery, although no one was crowned in the
narrow sense of the word. One may, however, accept the
renewal of the ancient Oath of Mount Ruetli as a kind of
crowning achievement for the defenders of Swiss freedom. Perhaps Mr. Orlop was correct in singling out a
leader on whom honors were heaped. That leader could
only be the provincial governor of Schwyz, Werner
Stauffacher. Today Stauffacher is among the leading national heroes of Switzerland. After the battle of Mount
Morgarten he was indeed the uncrowned ruler of the
free Swiss.

The disaster at Mount Morgarten was not the only unexpected reverse for the proud Habsburgs. Seven years
later, the continuing war between King Louis and King
Frederick came to a head and in a final battle at Muehl-

dorf on the River Inn in Bavaria, Frederick not only lost
his throne and army, but was himself taken prisoner. For
the first time in the family's proud history, a Habsburg
King became the helpless pawn of his opponent. Louis
of Bavaria treated his fallen enemy well, keeping him
under conditions far removed from dungeons. His only
demand was that Frederick denounce his claims to the
German crown. After three years of imprisonment, Frederick was ready to renounce his claims to the German
crown so long as his victorious opponent would acknowledge the Habsburgs in their own lands. He knew very
well that it would be difficult to sell such a settlement
to his belligerent brothers, Albert, Leopold and Otto, so
he asked Louis to allow him his conditional freedom for
the purpose of convincing his brothers to lay down their
arms.

Frederick's proposition was heartily welcomed by the
battle-scarred Louis. He gave his royal prisoner a few
knights to see him safely back to his own lands, with
the understanding that if Frederick failed to convince
Albert and Leopold to lay down their arms and make
peace, he was to return voluntarily to the Bavarian's
custody. The emotional upsets of the election and subsequent idleness had undermined Frederick's health and
a somewhat weak constitution also contributed to his de-
cline, but the mission ahead was too important to be
avoided.

When he reached Vienna, he was hailed as the "rightful" Emperor, but Frederick soon realized that his job
wasn't going to be an easy one. Leopold, still smarting
from his unexpected defeat at Morgarten, would have no
part of his brother's peace plan. Otto felt the same about
it and if anything, wanted to step up the war. After a
few weeks of bickering, a saddened Frederick returned

to Germany and imprisonment despite his brothers' solemn assurance that a word given under duress need not be honored. Even the Pope sent a message assuring Frederick he was under no obligation to return to prison under the circumstances, but Frederick went back anyway. Louis the Bavarian was so overwhelmed with Frederick's honesty that he offered him coregency in the Empire even if the Habsburg brothers were to continue the struggle. Frederick was much moved by the offer. His greatest enemy was treating him far better than his own family. What strange quirk of fate had given him hope for the Imperial crown, yet not quite enough hope? The pattern of giving with one hand and taking with the other, which seems inherent in the old curse, was clear once again. One more electoral vote and all this might not have happened! And now, with the chance of corule at hand, Frederick's brother Otto was in revolt against him again. Otto always picked the worst time to hurt his brother. While Frederick had been fighting Louis, Otto had risen against him in the belief that he had been done out of his share of the paternal inheritance. Forming a coalition with two enemies of Austria, the King of Bohemia and the King of Hungary, and with auxiliary troops from those two foreign nations, he had invaded Austria to make his claims known. Frederick, still unable to cope with his German claims, had no choice but to surrender to his own brother and in deepest humiliation turn over the city and castle of Hainburg and part of the Austrian revenues to Otto.

The opportunity for a peaceful solution passed and with it went all hope for even a partial rule of the German Empire. The struggle continued until Duke Leopold died in 1326, opening the way for a peace treaty at last. As if possessed by the furies, the surviving brothers, Otto and

Albert, went to war against the other over the inheritance while Frederick looked on from his imprisonment in far-off Bavaria.

Finally, in 1330 everything was settled and peace came to the Habsburg lands. But for Frederick, released by Louis, it came too late. The emotional turmoil had caused another breakdown and he withdrew to his estate at Gutenstein. There, within days after the great reconciliation, he died and was buried in the monastery of Mauerbach which he had founded some years before. It should be noted that neither Leopold nor Frederick lived beyond the age of thirty—even in those times an early age to die.

To the last, Frederick did not understand why fate had been so unkind to him. An excellent ruler as rulers go, the young man had done nothing to deserve such tragedy. The great Austrian historian Hugo Hantsch puts it this way in his *History of Austria.*

"Thus, a tragic fate had turned the proud and courageous fighter into a tired and weak man shattered in body and soul, who countered the fate he could not understand in the only way left to him: the highest acceptance of God's hand. But the succession of misfortune was far from over."

Professor Hantsch refers to the "unexplained" misfortunes of Duke Albert, Frederick's successor.

Since Frederick had left no heirs, the rule fell upon his younger brother, Albert, the fifth of that name to reign in the Habsburg lands. But because a new line had started with the division of the Habsburg properties, he was called Albert II of that line.

Albert inherited nothing but defeat on his accession. Originally trained to be a priest, he had no stomach for the business of politics. Austria lay badly scarred from civil war, the coffers were empty, the German throne seemed further away than ever, and all Albert could hope for was to restore his territories to something of their former glory. Thus, Albert seemed destined to become the first peaceful Habsburg to rule. He might have been successful in this role and well liked by his own people, had not fate played him a dirty trick.

Shortly after his enthronement, he fell ill after a banquet. At first the trouble seemed to be indigestion, but several days afterwards, unmistakable signs of something far more sinister appeared. He could not walk straight, and his physicians diagnosed his ailment as poisoning. But why would anyone want to poison the peaceful young prince? Because he was a Habsburg, a name synonymous with conquest and greed.

Nothing the physicians tried would help Albert's unfortunate condition. Mindful of what happened to an earlier bearer of his name when he was poisoned, Albert did not allow himself to be strung up by his feet to drain the poison. Besides, it was too late. He was lame, and as "Albert the Lame" he entered the ranks of history. Soon he could do business only from his armchair, and word of his affliction spread around Europe. Rumors pointed to the Habsburg prince as "having been struck down by God for his sins"—perhaps hereditary—and Albert's political power was as restricted as his movements. From the first weeks of his accession and the unfortunate affliction to his death in 1358 he never left his armchair again. His mind was unaffected by the poison which made his imprisonment for life even more unbearable, and he could not understand why fate had brought him this misfortune. Finally he was forced to turn over the reigns of government to his brother Otto.

Despite his illness, Albert must be counted as among the most worthy of the Habsburg rulers of Austria. His reign was a peaceful one and perhaps his greatest deed was the creation of a new order of succession for the House of Austria. Mindful of the tragic end of his father, Albert I, at the hands of another Habsburg prince, Albert II decreed that henceforth all sons of the Habsburgs must rule together jointly and with equal rights and that nobility and citizens were to witness this decision and must never support one brother against the other. Shortly thereafter, he died from his mysterious illness, and his son, Rudolph IV, who was barely nineteen years old succeeded him.

Rudolph IV was called The Founder because he started the University of Vienna and contributed materially to the erection of Saint Stephen's Cathedral in the capital. But then he also contributed a forged document to Austrian history known as the "Minor Privilege," a document establishing Austria as something apart from all other countries.

Rudolph had hoped that Austria would now at last become one of the German electorates in view of its rapid rise to fame and importance within the German Empire. But the seven original German electors were in no hurry to add an eighth to their number, and Austria's rise in power was by no means a reason for doing so. Far from it. If anything, the importance of Austria at that time argued against the German electors raising the rank of Austria's rulers. Piqued by this slight, Rudolph decided to go the German electors one better. He decreed that being an elector wasn't really all that great and that the House of Austria had superior rank. The "Minor Privilege" referred to the Habsburgs as the hereditary archmasters of the hunt of the German Empire as well as archdukes of the Palatinate and dukes of Suevia—all three nonexistent titles of his own creation. (Rudolph was truly an imaginative man. Besides inventing the "Minor Privilege," he also "discovered" a previously unknown early Habsburg saint named Saint Morandus.) However, the idea of becoming archdukes of Austria instead of just plain dukes did not take hold immediately, and it wasn't until the following century that Duke Ernest, The Iron, father of Emperor Frederick III, decided he needed something extra to support his waning might. This fifteenth-century monarch was the first one to remember Rudolph's imaginative creation of the title and decided to call himself officially "Archduke" of Austria.

With these ideas of expansion going on in his mind, if not in reality, Rudolph cast a jealous eye towards the successful renaissance princes of nearby Italy. He felt himself akin to them, their grandiose view of the world, their relationship with the re-emerging cultures of antiquity. The young prince had a romantic notion of his family's destiny. At the age of nineteen, he already felt he might some day combine the Germanic lands once ruled by his great namesake with the sunny Italian provinces he loved and thus restore the fabulous concept of Charlemagne. For that reason, he spent much time with Italian potentates, courting their favor and inviting them to become his allies.

In the seventh year of his reign, he accepted an invitation of the powerful Duke of Milan to visit with him.

This was the more fortunate as Barbanas Visconti had an unmarried daughter named Viridis. Rudolph's brother Leopold was eligible and most willing to marry her for the sake of the Habsburg family cause, and Rudolph was to arrange it on his trip to Italy. Another reason for his visit was the increasing power of the Patriarch of Aquileia which threatened Austria's southern flank.

During the weeks in Milan, Rudolph spoke incessantly of the classical dream of a united Empire, and as a first step towards that dream, he convinced the Duke of Milan that something should be done to curb the Patriarch.

At a state dinner in honor of the betrothed couple, Rudolph felt himself at the height of success. Toast after toast was offered by the illustrious Italian nobility present. It was a hot day and the drinks chilled. Apparently, Rudolph had inherited the Habsburg weakness towards sudden colds, or perhaps the nearby swamps of the Po had provided a poisonous insect, but in any event, the young man fell ill the next day and had to postpone his journey home. He developed a high fever, and there was little the doctors could do to help. Within twenty-four hours after taking to bed, Rudolph was dead at age twenty-six.

Once again, the "insidious Habsburg curse" had struck down one of the family at the moment of greatest triumph, unexpectedly and suddenly.

Although Rudolph's achievements on the real plane are not particularly significant in the long view of history, his cultural contributions to the unfoldment of Austria cannot be overlooked. The historian Adam Wandruszka considers Rudolph the originator of the Habsburg mythos, the romanticized mystique of the divine mission of the Habsburgs, the House of Austria, as leaders of Europe, a supernational and perhaps supernaturally orig-

inated family with special privileges, special rights and
sometimes special duties:

"The belief in a mission and special role of the House
of Habsburg Rudolph, who died without issue, left to the
later Habsburgs together with his immense ambitions
which included Bohemia, Hungary, as well as Italy and
the Rhineland, and above all the Imperial Crown. . . .
Rudolph IV, the founder of the Habsburg myth, the belief in the rightful claim of the dynasty to royal office."

Rudolph's unexpected death at age twenty-six shocked
his contemporaries. As far as the Austrian lands were concerned, the death left them in the hands of two dissimilar
boys, fifteen-year-old Albert and fourteen-year-old Leopold. As they grew older, the difference between them
became so strong that it became impossible to maintain
the common rule of Habsburg possessions decreed by
Rudolph IV. Eventually the lands were divided between
the two with the elder, Albert, retaining Austria proper
and Leopold, the rest, including the original Habsburg
possessions in Switzerland, or what was now left of them.

While the Habsburgs were busily engaged in trying to
increase their might in Austria and northern Italy, the
Swiss were just as busily determining to get rid of them.
Gradually, other parts of Switzerland joined the emerg-
ing Swiss federation. The powerful city of Zurich even
fought a war against the Habsburgs to a standstill but
lost whatever they had gained in the ensuing peace
arrangement.

Lucerne, rich city on the lake of the same name and a
close neighbor of the three Swiss cantons, yearned to be
free of the Habsburg yoke. In view of the difficulties
the Habsburg princes found themselves in, the city fathers of Lucerne thought that the time was at hand to

attempt a break for freedom. Occupying several nearby strong points in the closing days of 1385, they concluded a defense alliance with the strong town of Sempach. Situated not far from Lake Lucerne in the hilly country of central Switzerland, Sempach, on the shore of a small lake originally called the Sursee but nowadays referred to as Lake Sempach, was to become another crucial milestone in the destruction of Habsburg power in Switzerland, their ancient home.

V A Visit with the Dead of Sempach

The third location I had decided to visit in the company
of my psychic associate Arthur Orlop was the area of the
Battle of Sempach. I had picked this location because it
was here that the Habsburgs received their next-to-final
blow in their expulsion from Switzerland. What happened at Sempach could not have been anticipated or
prevented. As is my custom, I did not acquaint myself
with the details of this important battle or with its geographical location. I merely requested that Mario Hefner
drive on to the area of the battle. Long before we reached
the part of Switzerland involved in this historical event, I
studied the last drawing Mr. Orlop had given me that
morning. According to this drawing, we were to come
down a main road, past several buildings, then turn left
into what he described as a private sandy road curving
around a large field, then past some sort of building and
eventually wind up on an even smaller path. In the distance we would notice the towers of an overland electric
supply line. The drawing was in the main accurate as I
was able to determine later on when we arrived at our
destination.

We were riding through open countryside now, once

in a while passing through a village or a small town. Mr. Orlop didn't seem to be too interested in the landscape. Frequently, he would mumble something to himself. Eventually, my ear caught some words pertaining to our next location, and I decided to see whether I might perhaps get some advance impressions of the place we were to visit shortly. I, myself, hadn't the slightest idea what it looked like and even Mr. Hefner had not been there before. Thus, there was no visual image even in our unconscious from which the psychic could draw information.

"We will have to stop eventually at a spot where the main road and a private road meet," Mr. Orlop explained. "We will enter this private road and pass some private houses on the left while to the right we will observe the towers of an overland high-voltage line. We will see a towerlike structure of great antiquity partially broken off. Then there is a sandy path and a farmhouse to the right. The path continues to a meadow on the right and past some small houses on the left. We have just been to a castle," Mr. Orlop continued, referring to the Habsburg Castle we had visited earlier that morning. "But this time we are not heading toward any kind of castle or fortress. We are going to visit a farmhouse."

Two hours later I knew that he had described the landscape exactly as we were to find it—as if he had been hovering above it and had looked down upon it from a bird's-eye view. But now we were still at least an hour's ride away from our destination.

"What is the significance of our next goal?" I inquired.

"Someone, like the owner of the territory, had to leave the area in great haste. I also get the impression that a relative of the vulture family bearing another name, however, is connected with this. This man had something to do with foreign politics on an ambassadorial or similar level."

"What country did this politician come from?"

"I feel I'd like to go in the direction of Austria."

"What else can you tell me about this man?"

"I get the feeling he was interested in better Swiss-Austrian trade. He was a nobleman, married to a noble-woman. I am trying to get his name for you. Her name sounds like Vollwerk or Stolberg or something like it. I can't get his."

For a while Mr. Orlop fell silent. Suddenly I saw a towerlike building come up on the right side of the road. It looked exactly the way the psychic had described it earlier. The description was completely accurate, even to the fact that the tower was partly broken off at the top. Shortly after, we saw the sandy path of which Mr. Orlop had spoken. Now we found ourselves in the center of a farm area covered by large numbers of apple or-chards and occasional farmhouses. As we turned a bend in the road, we could clearly see the high-voltage towers Mr. Orlop had spoken of. The two of us decided to leave the car and walk the rest of the way with Mr. Hefner fol-lowing us in the car. Apparently, Mr. Orlop did not know exactly where to stop to get his deepest impression, and so I merely followed along waiting for him to decide which way we should go.

"I hear people yelling on top of that hill," he remarked suddenly. "This path will become narrower and around the bend you will no longer be able to drive the car."

Sure enough, we reached a point where the car had to stay behind and Mr. Hefner joined us on foot.

A few minutes later we found ourselves at the edge of a dense wood. Advancing hesitantly, Mr. Orlop pointed at the trees and said, "After dark you just can't walk here."

"What do you mean can't?" I demanded.

"Because you would encounter *them*."

"What exactly do you feel here at the edge of the woods?"

"I see, clairvoyantly that is, a man not too tall with bulging eyeballs. His face is red. He wears old-fashioned striped trousers torn half-way down the leg in a jagged fashion."

I was fascinated by his description. The uniform of the Swiss soldiery during the Battle of Sempach, the exact spot where we now stood, fitted pretty closely the description given by Mr. Orlop. He, of course, had no idea where we were.

"What happened in this area, Mr. Orlop?" I asked as casually as I could. The question shook him up.

"Oh God," he said covering his eyes with his hands as if he wanted to shut out some terrible sight. "What didn't happen here? First of all, the man I see must have been one of them. He also wears a hunter's hat with a kind of feather. Instead of sandals or shoes he wears pointed boots, something I find particularly unusual. That is to say, the fact that they are so sharply pointed. He carries an ax and a halberd. But behind him I sense a man running. A thin man with a curved nose. The other fellow is carrying a shovel and sticks. Those are the only ones I feel so far."

"Keep looking. Keep looking," I encouraged the psychic.

"I sense four more men carrying a strange contraption, like the lower part of a coffin to put bodies onto," Mr. Orlop continued with a shudder.

Again I reiterated my question as to what exactly had transpired in this area.

"I think an entire clan was wiped out here, a large group of people."

"Can you get anything else about the events here?"

"A lot of killing has taken place here. I get the impression of a man from abroad who had come here and been made a resident of the area subject to a larger city. Prior to his coming, the small community had been on its own. I get the feeling of a warlike action, but more of a peasant war or a peasant's rebellion between the local peasants and the lords in their fortresses. The peasants demanded some of the castles around and from that developed this warlike action."

"How did it all end?"

"They concluded a kind of agreement. The people received more land and certain rights regarding the castles, too. However, this agreement has to be ratified by the high council first."

"Who won this action in the end?"

"Well, among the peasants there were also noblemen, that is to say, individuals who could not call themselves noblemen but who were like that. It was a question of the people—the peasants—overcoming the power of the castles. I think that some of these noblemen who were reduced to peasantry by the loss of their castles were holed up here, and they were hoping to get some of their rights restored by the high council. Until that happened, they were going to hold out and defend themselves. Of the nobility that had come to this spot, more than half lost their lives. This was all part of a Swiss civil war or a war between peasants and nobility."

We began to walk back towards the car. Nothing in this peaceful landscape in the height of summer indi-

cated that a ferocious battle had taken place here at
one time, for there were no signposts pointing to the bat-
tlegrounds. As yet, Mr. Orlop had no idea where he was.
I questioned him about this because I wondered whether
he got the impression of a name or date or something
that would identify our present location. He thought
about it for a moment and then said, haltingly, "I get
something like Semson. It sounds like that. I am sure of
the first three letters, S-E-M."

A little later we stood on a hill crowned by a small
church. Behind it was a simple monument inscribed to
the heroes of the Battle of Sempach. It was then that Mr.
Orlop learned for the first time where he had just been.

Much of what had come through the medium made
sense to me later in the light of further research. The
year 1385 had been filled with mounting tension between
the rich city of Lucerne and her Habsburg overlords.
The majority of the Lucerne high council was determined
to break away from Austrian domination, awaiting only
the proper opportunity to do so. Only a small minority
still sided with the foreign overlords. All around them,
the people of Lucerne could see the free Swiss run their
own affairs. Across the lake the three original cantons of
Uri, Schwyz and Unterwalden enjoyed freedom from
Habsburg domination, and the people of Lucerne thought
they were entitled to the same. In the last days of the
year they felt themselves strong enough to occupy the
nearby town of Rotenburg, which was indispensable to
their defense. A few days later the citizen army of Lucerne destroyed Castle Wolhusen occupied by a Habsburg garrison and immediately concluded a defensive
alliance with the nearby town of Sempach. This was
enough of a challenge to the Habsburgs, and Duke Leo-

pold II decided to reply by amassing an army as quickly as he could. Because of the conditions of the fourteenth century, it was almost a half a year before it could come to a decisive battle, but on July 9, 1386, the Austrian Army, led by a number of local Swiss noblemen fighting on the Habsburg side, moved along the small lake Sursee, towards the town of Sempach. Once Sempach was taken, the road to Lucerne would be open. It was a pretty mixed army consisting of Austrians, Germans, some Swiss and even professional mercenaries, and Italian auxiliaries. Opposing them was not only Lucerne, but the three original cantons as well with an army numbering two thousand men.

While the Swiss were lightly armored, if at all, and used the halberd as their main weapon, the Austrian knights, heavily armored and rather clumsy on their horses, had to rely on long spears and swords. Under the circumstances, they were easily outmaneuvered by the more mobile Swiss. At first, however, the Austrians managed to inflict some losses on the enemy simply because they were better trained, but when the sun came up on that very hot summer day, the tides turned in favor of the Swiss. Between the heat and the heavy armor, the cavaliers found themselves hard pressed, the Austrian flag was pulled down and trampled upon, and panic set in. A soldier cried, "Save yourself, Austria. Save yourself," and hearing it, preferring death to flight, Duke Leopold himself dismounted and, followed by his staff, joined the fray. A moment later Austria's ruler was dead. When the nobility saw their duke sprawled in his own blood, confusion set in, but the battle was far from over, for about this time a man by the name of Arnold Winkelried turned the scales definitely in favor of the free Swiss. Rushing against a solid front of mounted knights, he seized a number of their spears, and thrust them into his own body. His action distracted the knights just long enough and opened a wedge just large enough for the Swiss to lunge into the midst of the remaining knights and thus win the Battle of Sempach.

The Austrian Army and their allies fled in total confusion back towards the north. Sixteen hundred and seventy-six Austrians were left behind dead in the battlefield, including four hundred knights. Only 120 Swiss had lost their lives. On the Austrian side, the defeat was blamed on bad organization, and heat and treason. Again it seemed incredible how a well-planned campaign led by experienced military men following all the rules of warfare could so suddenly and unexpectedly fall victim to nearly total destruction. It almost seemed as if something stronger than human ability or error was involved.

What Mr. Orlop had clairvoyantly relived at the edge of the battlefield appeared to have been a part of the action only. His accurate description of the Swiss uniform of that period, his mention of the high council and the need to pass on certain arrangements were details he could not have been familiar with, but I found them entirely correct in the light of my later historical research. It is, of course, quite possible that some restless spirits of men killed in this battle could not find peace and entrance into the next dimension and are forever roaming the bloodstained woods on the edge of the battlefield of Sempach.

Frankly, if I were an Austrian, or even some other foreigner, I wouldn't walk that sandy path at the edge of the woods either after dark. The Swiss are a fierce freedom-loving people and know how to handle an ax or a halberd like no one else.

When things had quieted down, the Habsburgs dispatched messengers to carry the body of Duke Leopold from the battleground at Sempach and bury it properly in hallowed ground. Curiously enough, they chose the abbey at Koenigsfelden in Switzerland as his last resting place. The abbey itself had been built on the spot where Duke Albert I had been murdered back in 1308, and thus the bodies of grandfather and grandson were united in death as Habsburg power dwindled more and more in the very land from whence the family had come. For a few years the Habsburgs managed to hold on to their Swiss and southwest German possessions.

But when Emperor Frederick III, "Frederick with the empty pocket," as he was called—the son and successor of the slain Leopold—was placed on the list of outcasts by the Pope for having backed an anti-pope, John XXIII, the free Swiss used this as an excuse to seize what was left of the Habsburg dominions in Switzerland. They occupied the entire Aargau, including the castle itself. Finally, after 1415 the Habsburgs were reduced to Austria and a few scattered estates in the Rhineland, but Switzerland was in essence free of their domination.

One would think that common sense would dictate at least some wise decision, some successful enterprise, even under the heavy cloud of a curse. But not so with Frederick III, called by historians the "Archdunderhead of the Empire." We have his own diary to help us understand this enigmatic man. Writing of the fourteenth century and his antecedents, Frederick said, "The flag of Austria was not victorious. My ancestors have been defeated under this flag three times." He was, of course, referring to the disaster at Morgarten, the battle Frederick II had lost at Nuehldorf and, above all, Sempach and the death of Leopold. Despite this dismal state of affairs in the previous century, he did nothing to improve upon matters in his own time. His attitude could be summed up in the simple phrase, "Who wants to win victory? I'll be glad to survive."

Perhaps Frederick was being held back from any kind of positive action by something more powerful than he himself could cope with. Misfortune after misfortune came his way.

True, he was not only an Archduke of Austria, but also the German Emperor and therefore in rank superior to his brother Albert VI. But Albert was the opposite of Frederick. Where Frederick hesitated, Albert struck. The mayor of Vienna showed a conciliatory attitude towards Frederick even though his oath of allegiance had originally been to Albert. When the Viennese revolted because Frederick was doing nothing to protect them against marauding Hungarians and highwaymen on their own roads, Frederick, rather than face the deputation sent to see him, simply up and left the city. As soon as he had gone, the city fathers locked the gates in case he should change his mind and come back.

But the mayor had to pay dearly for having been kind to Frederick. By order of Albert VI, he was drawn and quartered in a public square. Albert was definitely no weakling.

Meanwhile, Frederick set up headquarters at nearby Wiener Neustadt, a little fortress town south of Vienna. He no longer had a real army since most of the better knights had gone over to his brother Albert or found something to do abroad, so he decided to hire some mercenaries. Unfortunately, he never figured out how to pay them since the treasury was empty. After a while the mercenaries (who had nothing to do either) revolted against him because he could not pay them. His brother Albert VI then decided to seize the capital city of Vienna. Instead of demanding the return of his proud residence, Frederick awaited an opportune moment to regain entry. When Albert left for the south, Frederick re-entered without fanfare. Eventually, however, he had to leave again, for Matthias, King of Hungary, decided to take over the eastern portion of Austria. Frederick did nothing to stop him.

Then, with all his other difficulties, a blood condition forced Frederick to seek the help of his physicians, who amputated one of his legs. It became impossible for him to travel, with the result he found himself confined to his private apartments, wherever they might be at any given moment.

He became more and more withdrawn and spent many hours a day writing the mysterious letters, A, E, I, O, U for *"Austria Est Imperare Orbi Universo,"* on pieces of parchment. The meaning of that medieval Latin phrase is "All the world is subject to Austria," the phrase that became the motto of his illustrious house. A more ironical device he could not have thought up. To be fair to Fred-

erick, though, he did travel to Rome and was crowned
by the Pope, the only Habsburg who did so. But in the
latter part of the fifteenth century the gesture was already
meaningless. The Habsburgs had finally hit bottom. Their
power was low; they were disunited; their reputation
was gone; and their male members were beset by misfortunes and illness. Had the ancient curse finally hit its
mark?

Frederick's answer to all the misfortunes of his long
reign was to "survive his enemies." That was all he dared
hope. The Viennese used to walk underneath his windows (when he was in residence, that is) and sing, *"Er
sass also still und sah nur zu—er fragte nit wie oder wu."*
("He just sat there quietly and looked on—he never
asked how or what was done.") It was simply a matter of
destiny to him. But so virulent had been the workings of
the ancient curse in the life of Frederick, that it seems
the anger was spent for a while. When he died of old
age, or perhaps because the infection that had earlier
caused him the loss of a leg had finally reached higher,
he saw at least the signs of better times ahead for his
children.

But we must remember that for a curse to hit with
surprise and topple the mighty from the heights just as
they begin to enjoy that position, heights must first be
climbed. At the moment the Habsburgs were at bottom.
Thus, it appears to me that the elevation of the next ruler
was still part of the scheme that had originated with the
accursed member of the house.

Frederick III was followed by his brilliant son Maximilian I. The Habsburg fortunes rose again, partially
through fortunate marriages, partially as a result of political and military campaigns. Maximilian managed to
live a reasonably successful life. There is nothing in his

rule one could ascribe to the workings of a curse or un-usual misfortune. Perhaps the only thing along the lines of a sinister hand of fate was the fact that his only son Philip died far too soon, leaving as heir that great European Charles V, who united both west and east and even the possessions beyond the seas in the greatest combination of lands and power ever held together by a single man. But Philip had married Joanna the Mad of Spain, and with this marriage there entered into the Habsburg bloodstream the destructive seed of the insane Spanish inheritance.

However, everything seemed to be going right for once when Charles V came to power. The brilliant young man combined in his person the considerable statesmanship of the Habsburg family with the mystical deeper understanding of his royalty inherited from his mother. On the worldly level he ruled over more territory than any Habsburg had up to that time, in fact, more land than any one man ever had in Europe. The riches of the new world that came with the Spanish inheritance opened new vistas of greatness, new expansion and new hope for an ancient family. But the breathing spell was short lived. Already the sinister hand of fate was silhouetted against the sky. As the years went on Charles was forced to split up his empire to obey the family law of split rule. Thus, the Spanish half of the Empire fell to the hands of Philip II while the Germanic half became the domain of Ferdinand and later his son Maximilian II. With the German half came the Imperial crown, now a matter of tradition rather than left to the vicarious choice of the electors. It would take extraordinary circumstances to take the Imperial crown from the Habsburgs again. Still, one could hardly call the division into two halves of the Habsburg Empire the workings of an ancient curse. To the contrary, one might take it as an administrative step dictated by necessity. But the religious peace of Augsburg forced upon Emperor Charles in 1555 foreshadowed all the difficulties yet to come, including the most disastrous civil war Europe had ever encountered in her long history.

Dissent between the two lines of the family began at an early stage. Philip II turned into a fanatic Catholic despot while Ferdinand continued to live the easy-going life of an Austrian trying to maintain what was his while at the same time avoiding conflict wherever possible. Under the administrative division, Ferdinand was supposed to name his nephew Philip as his successor to the Imperial crown as well, but he never lived up to that promise. Instead, the liberal-thinking, almost Protestant, Maximilian II became Ferdinand's successor, dividing the two lines of the Habsburgs even further, and with division came weakness. At the very height of their apparent success, the Habsburgs received one blow after the other. Philip II came close to uniting Britain with Continental Europe through his marriage with Mary Tudor. But that marriage remained childless and Mary herself died shortly after.

Charles V was a wise man, though he saw how his high-flung scheme of world dominion was crumbling at the edges. He had done what he could, but now he could do no more. Consequently, he divested himself of his powers one by one until nothing remained to him but the Imperial crown. Traditionally, that crown cannot be resigned but must be worn by its bearer until the moment of death. The last days of his life Charles V spent in a specially constructed annex to the monastery of San Yuste. The act of resignation itself, spread as it was over a period of months and encompassing the lands he ruled, made a tremendous impression on the people of Europe. If so powerful and so glorious a prince as Charles V could not enjoy his might to the very end, how vain and shallow was that power after all. But the shadows of melancholy were not totally alien to Charles V either. Somehow he felt that he could not withstand the hand of fate, and he chose to die like a monk rather than a prince.

Maximilian II, who succeeded Ferdinand in the Germanic lands and in Austria, also felt the heavy hand of an unkind fate on his shoulder. Married to Maria, the fanatically Catholic sister of the fanatically Catholic King Philip of Spain, he spent a lifetime trying to live with a wife who disagreed with him on almost all levels. But it had been a dynastic marriage following in the tradition that the Habsburgs must intermarry as often as possible to maintain their power and pure royal blood. In the end, this policy of intermarriage turned many of them into idiots or at least into weak and incapable rulers. But even outside his family life Maximilian was thwarted at every step. Twice he tried to obtain the crown of Poland for himself and twice he failed. On one occasion, he rebelled against his own father, Ferdinand, and was mercilessly put down. In the end, his own liberal leanings towards religious peace, if not Protestantism, failed to jell and Maximilian spent his last remaining days a frustrated, embittered man.

His brother-in-law Philip II of Spain was not sleeping on a bed of roses, either. After initial success and the grandeur that came with the possession of the overseas territories, Philip was suddenly faced with the fact that his son and heir, Don Carlos, was not only incapable to succeed him due to madness, but had apparently also engaged in correspondence with the Dutch rebels and perhaps treasonable offences. Whatever the situation, when the facts became clear to the King, he himself arrested his son and ordered him confined to his quarters to his last day. Whether Don Carlos died as a result of insanity or whether he was put to death on orders of his own father, we will never know.

Philip of Spain regarded himself the chosen leader of his people who must not mingle with the common folk because that would lessen the majesty of the monarchy. He was sure that God was on his side, and that the extreme measures he took against the rebels in the Netherlands and the dissenters at home were justified because of his favored position at the right side of God. His critics pointed to the needless cruelty with which he murdered large numbers of Protestants in his domains and with which his generals suppressed the natural national ambitions of the people of Belgium and Holland. At the same time Philip feared his victories and frequently interfered with his own generals lest they tempt God's hand too much by pursuing the enemy or taking good advantage of a victory. Philip had an almost mystical understanding that God was watching him very closely. Whether or not he knew of the ancient curse is hard to establish now, but he had a firm feeling that a Habsburg King could not undertake anything without being called to account for it before a superior tribunal. At the height of his political success, when it appeared that Spain would be the dominating world power in the century to come, a combination of bad management and storms destroyed the proud Spanish fleet. With the end of the Spanish Armada and England's victory, the balance of power shifted irreversibly to the west, and Britain rose to world dominance, not Spain.

In Germany and Austria Rudolph II had succeeded his father Maximilian II. From the very outset, Rudolph's dislike for politics made him a most unlikely choice to hold things together at a time when a firm hand was needed at the rudder. The upcoming struggle between Catholics and Protestants, already deepening every day, required a firm decision to make things livable between them. Instead, Rudolph withdrew more and more into the world of fine art and the occult, leaving the government in professional political hands, but they were hands that lacked the fine touch of diplomacy so necessary to keep things in balance at such a difficult time. Gradually, a cleavage developed between Rudolph and his brother Matthias. Matthias felt himself more suitable to rule than Rudolph and eventually made good his claims.

Ultimately, war broke out between the two brothers, and Matthias occupied Prague, Rudolph's residence, forcing his Imperial brother to live like a prisoner in his shadow. Rudolph died heirless shortly afterwards, leaving a shattered empire to his conqueror. The spectacle of the two brothers fighting each other in open battle and in the political arena had horrified Europe for many years. Now Rudolph was gone, and hope sprang up again that a unified Empire with firm policies might result.

But Matthias could not stem the onrolling tide of hatred and inflexibility. The Thirty Years' War was in the not-too-distant future. During his short reign, he was as frustrated with the German princes and the nobility in his own land as had been Rudolph.

At his death, Matthias, like Rudolph before him, left no heir, for his wife, Queen Anna, could not bear children.

Thus, by an ironic twist of fate there came to the throne a man who was least likely to reconcile the two opposing parties—a fanatic by the name of Ferdinand, who had been brought up by the Jesuits and who knew only one way of life: to exterminate the Protestants and to restore his lands to the fold of the Catholic Mother Church. To achieve this end, he would use whatever means were necessary.

On May 23, 1618, the students at Charles University in Prague had demanded the restoration of the ancient privileges taken from them by Imperial decree. Joined by a mob on the way up to the castle, they had entered the castle itself and in the excitement had thrown the two Imperial governors out the windows as a symbol of their break with the Habsburg government. The two governors landed on a large garbage heap and thus were not injured except in their pride. But Emperor Matthias had taken a dim view of this behavior, and as a result the first phase of the Thirty Years' War had begun. The Bohemian war dealt with the rebellion of Bohemia from the Habsburg Empire and ended in a bloodletting at the White Mountain two years later.

By now the intractable Ferdinand had succeeded his uncle Matthias, and he dealt with the captured Bohemian nobles in a most barbarous and cruel manner. All pretense at reconciliation between Protestants and Catholics was gone. The Habsburgs now stood firmly in the camp of reaction and suppression. Even though individual members of the family might have felt otherwise, house policy dictated the adherence to a stiff uncompromising line.

For thirty years, war and pestilence ravaged nearly all of central Europe. Failure to come to terms with the

Lutherans and the Calvinists brought foreigners onto German soil. Frenchmen and Swedes, Italians and Danes turned Germany into a near wasteland where the shells of burned-out cities remained for years as grim reminders of man's foolishness. According to contemporary figures, nearly one-third of the population of Europe was wiped out as a result of the Thirty Years' War. From the confiscated lands of the Protestant nobility, wherever the Catholic Habsburgs reigned, a new nobility was created and given the ancient lands with newly created titles. In this way, the Habsburgs hoped to draw this new class to themselves as servants of the state.

In the end, the fanatical Ferdinand died and was succeeded by his son, Ferdinand III, a young man tired of war, tired of pestilence, tired of destruction. He forced his own people and his enemies to make peace at last. Everyone was exhausted and economically destroyed, and things were pretty much the way they had been before the war had started as far as the two religions were concerned. Thus, the irony of this terrible war lay in its uselessness. What had led the Habsburg rulers into such a course of action?

Rather than come to realistic terms with their world, the Habsburgs encouraged an entire line of mystical involvements for their people. Various Catholics saints were restored to great prominence. A great mother of Austria was created in and around the pilgrimage church of Maria Zell, and the worship of physical symbols of Christianity by the population was encouraged as a means of drawing their attention away from harsh realities.

In other countries, the existence of a dynasty over long periods of time had led to stability and a sense of mature responsibility in the royal families. The Tudors of England felt themselves to be the divinely appointed first

servants of their people rather than the owners of a
country. The French kings were concerned with the glory
of France, the solidification of their borders, and the defense of what they had acquired rather than with the
glory of their family or the destiny of their family to rule.
As a result, both France and England were spared that
unhappy dissension between two strong opposing factions that had rent central Europe.

But when we examine the personal record of each
Habsburg ruler carefully and dispassionately, there appears a pattern from the early medieval days onward.
Despite temporary success and occasional periods of un-
disturbed power, there is always the downfall, the unexpected disaster, the surprise element not provided for,
not properly acted on. Whatever a particular Habsburg
prince built up, inevitably it fell apart either in his own
lifetime or under his successor. Again and again succeeding Habsburg princes had to do the same job over again
to maintain themselves. In their personal lives few, if
any of them, were happy because of the family's policy
of intermarriage that not one of them had as yet dared
to challenge.

When the year 1648 had written an end to the long
bloodletting, there was little respite in the offing. Already,
the menacing specter of the Turkish enemy rose in the
distance, but the Habsburgs were neither politically,
economically nor morally ready to cope with it.

The man who inherited what was left of the Holy Roman Empire and the Austrian House lands was hardly the most handsome of all princes. His long, curvy nose and his extraordinary protruding lip were pointed out by his contemporaries as a sure sign that the Habsburgs had finally fallen victim to total degeneration. As a matter of fact, Leopold I did represent the pure Habsburg image both physically and emotionally. He was a man who preferred inaction to aggressiveness; a man who believed that in time all things would come right by themselves, while at the same time firmly believing in the divine mission of the Habsburgs and their great destiny involving the future of Europe and in particular the defense of all Christendom against the heathens wherever they might be. That lofty ideal had gotten some very painful jolts during the previous reigns. After all, the Habsburgs were indirectly responsible for so much destruction in Europe that it took another generation and a half before it was back to any kind of normalcy and able to develop once again its better talents such as art and music. One cannot exonerate the Habsburgs from the holocaust and wholesale slaughter that was the Thirty Years' War.

They did not cause it by themselves, but they did not try
to stop it either. In their stubborn support for the Roman
Catholic Church they were, however, responsible for
the aggressive attitude of the Protestants. There is no
gainsaying what might have happened instead if the religious peace of Augsburg, which Emperor Charles V
disliked so much, had been actually implemented in the
following century instead of 1555, and Protestants and
Catholics been given equal rights all the way through.
Not a single Habsburg prince ever rose to demand such
action; even Maximilian II, who was friendly towards
the Protestants, was prevented by family pressures from
speaking out loud on behalf of religious peace.

The man who inherited this mess was not only ugly by
all physical standards, but he was ill prepared to become
Emperor to begin with. Brought up to become either an
artist or a churchman, or both, Leopold I did not involve
himself in affairs of state whenever he could possibly do
things more to his liking. After all, his brother, Ferdinand,
was destined to inherit the crown, but, unfortunately
Ferdinand died suddenly—even before his father, Ferdinand III—and by a stroke of fate, Leopold stepped into
the limelight.

This was not the only time when an heir presumptive
to the Austrian or German Imperial throne was removed unexpectedly, throwing the succession into less-
experienced hands. Time and again the heavy hand of
the curse seems to have shown itself in a strange chain
of events. Very few of the later Habsburgs were succeeded by their first-born sons. The majority either had
no sons or the sons predeceased them, leaving the succession in the hands of nephews or cousins.

The unexpected death of young Ferdinand was a bitter
blow, not only to his father, but to the Empire. The bril-

liant young man would have been just right to take on the increasing Turkish menace in the east and the intrigues of the French court in the west. Leopold, on the other hand, was a weak man who hated his job but grudgingly accepted it because there was no other way. The first thirty years of his reign were filled with a series of fruitless campaigns against the Turks.

Despite occasional victories in single engagements, matters came to a head in 1683 with the siege of Vienna by Turkish armies. At this point, all of Europe rallied to the Austrian cause because everyone knew that Vienna was the last bastion of the western world. If Vienna had been taken by the Turks, nothing could have stopped them from reaching the Atlantic. For the first time in European history the idea of a united Europe took shape. In the armies sent to help Leopold break the Turkish siege were contingents of many nationalities, including, even, Frenchmen and Englishmen, Italians, and a substantial Polish army under John Sobieski, who came upon the scene mounted on a white horse, the very image of the eleventh-hour savior. But as soon as the Turkish danger had run past its peak, dissension returned to the European princes. On the Austrian side a campaign was mounted to chase the Turks back into Turkey proper. It resulted in a partial conquest of Hungary, which had been all but lost to the Habsburgs in the previous period. But the pressures in the west were mounting. Forced to grant Hanover the electorate, thus bringing the number of electoral princes in Germany to nine, Leopold was also pressured into recognizing another king in Germany, the King of Prussia. The dissolution of the Holy Roman Empire was already plainly discernible on the horizon. There could not be two kings within one Germany, as Leopold well knew, but there was nothing he could do to stop the

Prussians from becoming the dominant power in central
Europe.

As a result of too many wars, the plague devastated
parts of Europe every few years. There were times when
Leopold could not even live in his capital city of Vienna,
and he took refuge where he was truly king. His music
and his love for the fine arts were the two areas in which
his inborn talents could develop freely, and he became
the composer of more than ninety operas, some of which
were actually performed at the theater. In view of contemporary, as well as later critics, Leopold the composer
was a man of substance and promise.

On one occasion, the Emperor was approached by a
fellow musician who was trying to express his enthusiasm
over a new opera he had just heard. He wondered if the
Emperor would not prefer to become a full-time composer and musician and leave matters of state to others.
With a sad but wise smile, Leopold is said to have replied, using the local dialect, "No, I don't think so, my
dear fellow. I'm doing better as Emperor."

Although his own rule had been anything but glorious
and although whatever victories had been fought and
won against the Turks were due to the genius of his generals, rather than himself, Leopold enjoyed a comparatively long reign and left two able sons, Joseph and
Charles, to look after what was left of the Habsburg Empire.

But even before he died in 1705, the old Emperor saw
his hopes of a united Habsburg Empire crumble once
again. Upon the death of the last Spanish Habsburg
prince, Charles II, in the year 1700, the Spanish and the
Austrian houses would have been combined to recreate
the ancient far-flung Empire as it had been in the six-
teenth century. It was precisely at this point that the

French produced a last will and testament allegedly written by Charles II leaving his possessions not to his natural cousins in Vienna, but to the French. The French King, named Philip V, was to take over in Spain, and as a result, the Spanish war of succession ensued. Although Leopold's younger son, Charles VI, went to Spain to try to save what the Habsburgs of Austria thought was their just inheritance, he was unsuccessful. The impoverished Habsburgs were in no position to prevail against the comparatively wealthy French, and Charles never ruled much of Spain. Meanwhile, his older brother, Joseph I, succeeded as Emperor and ruler of Austria. In Joseph, a singularly talented man came to the Habsburg throne. It looked as if the mistakes of the past would not be repeated, and reconciliation between Protestants and Catholics was in sight. Joseph did everything in his power to encourage peace between the two religious factions to the point where he got himself into a war with the Pope, the last war between Emperor and Pope ever fought. Joseph finally managed to force the Pope into submission, but it did the Habsburgs no good. Spain was lost, and to make things worse, Joseph himself—after only six years of rule and at the young age of thirty-three—fell victim to smallpox and died. To his contemporaries, the last great hope of the Habsburg dynasty died with him.

Since Joseph had left no heir, the Austrian and Holy Roman crown fell to his younger brother, Charles VI, who hurried home from Spain after hastily making peace with Philip V by abandoning almost everything the Habsburgs had hoped to retain. Fate had blessed him with only daughters, and he knew already that he would never have sons. His oldest daughter, Maria Theresa, was in line to inherit the throne, but such succession was against the accepted order, and Charles knew that he had to get the approval of the German electorate if he hoped to see Maria Theresa succeed him.

Charles spent most of his reign traveling about from court to court politely asking approval for his daughter to succeed him. In each case, of course, he had to pay a price for this exception to the rule, with the result that Austria had to give up all her rights in East India where a flourishing trade company had already made major inroads. Furthermore, in his bid for Maria Theresa's succession, he found himself involved in two wars he didn't care for—the Polish war of succession and a war against Turkey on the side of Prussia. In each case, Austria lost on all sides. In the end, however, the Emperor succeeded in getting approval for his daughter's succession from everyone in power with one exception. Bavaria would not sign on the dotted line. As soon as Charles had passed on and the reign of Maria Theresa had begun, the prince of Bavaria invaded Austria to claim what he considered a vacant throne.

In 1740 the male line of the House of Habsburg came to an end. The curse had found its mark. But had it ceased?

Maria Theresa had concluded a love match, something very rare in royal circles, with Francis, Duke of Lorraine. But before France would recognize either herself or her husband, Francis had to give up his country of Lorraine to the French and take a much less desirable territory to rule over, the Duchy of Tuscany in Italy. As it turned out, though, French approval of the succession of a daughter in the Habsburg domains and recognition of the so-called Pragmatic Sanction, the document allowing her to rule, was a hollow victory for Maria Theresa.

Since the Bavarian would not be party to it and was powerful enough to make war upon Austria, she had to fight for her rights anyway and defend them on the battlefield.

For forty years Maria Theresa was a motherly ruler of Austria and to a degree still maintained the fantasy of a Holy Roman Empire, although the German crown had become more and more hollow with the ascendancy of Prussia as the real power in Germany. Those forty years of rule were not without successes and improvements in government, to be sure, but the luck of the Habsburgs had apparently run out. If Charles of Bavaria had not died, perhaps the Habsburgs might not have continued beyond Maria Theresa, for hardly had the Bavarian danger passed than Prussia demanded a greater share of power in Germany. Taking advantage of Austria's weakened position, Frederick the Great invaded Silesia, until then an Austrian province, and conquered it. This loss was followed by other wars, all of which added to the impoverishment of the Habsburg Empire.

To make things even sadder for Maria Theresa, her beloved husband Francis died in 1765, and from that day on she never appeared in public without a black veil. What had kept this remarkable woman going in times of disaster was her own inner strength, which she certainly possessed to a great extent. Early in her career when she was in danger and her own counselors did not know whether to advise her to run for her life or stay, she looked up at them and asked, "What kind of faces are these at a time when it is necessary not to discourage the poor Queen but to help her and advise her?"

Despite her setbacks and personal tragedy, for a while it looked as if Maria Theresa could nevertheless rally the Habsburg cause once again and return Austria to the fold of major European powers. But her son and heir, Joseph II, saw things differently from his mother. Despite Maria Theresa's desire to reform and rejuvenate the government machinery and despite her humility and more liberal view of an Empress' destiny, she was still a conservative and faithful to the Church-supporting policies of the Habsburgs. Joseph was a Free Mason, a reformer, a rebel, and his philosophy radically differed from that of his mother. In later years, the tension between mother and son became more and more pronounced.

But Joseph could not put into action his sweeping reforms until after his mother's death. For the time being, all he could do was to chafe at the bit, speak of his future plans and raise eyebrows among the princes in Germany and even among the nobility of his own lands. No Habsburg had ever behaved the way Joseph was behaving. Naturally, this attitude troubled Maria Theresa, but she was powerless to change her son's views. What made any thought of a rebellious philosophy even more painful was the predicament of Marie Antoinette, Maria Theresa's daughter who was Queen of France, and the French Revolution. Never before had anything like the Revolution occurred in Europe. The tribunals of the French radicals were far from Austria's borders, but her own son Joseph evidently championed the cause of liberalism and who was to tell where it would all end?

Any speculation as to whether the Habsburg curse ended with the death of the last male member of the family must be laid aside when one examines the record of the succeeding House of Habsburg-Lorraine. The same succession of temporary victories followed by sudden and unexpected downfalls, the same irony of fate that removed the few capable members of the family from power while allowing incompetent Habsburgs long periods of domination, the same pattern of slow but sure destruction of a noble family is evident all the way through the later years of the dynasty when it continued to rule Austria and the surrounding territories even though the German crown was lost early in the nineteenth century.

Joseph II came to sole rule upon the death of his mother, Maria Theresa, in 1780. In the eleven years of his rule he managed to upend everything from religion to government. So ill prepared was his country to accept these reforms that the Emperor found nothing but hostility where he had expected open arms. Although he simplified the system of government and streamlined democracy so that more people could have more benefits from it, the age-old system was preferred over his modern, practical way of government.

Joseph stopped at nothing. No taboo was too sacred to be broken. Outlawing slavery, which under the name of serfdom still existed in Europe at that time, he went so far as to mingle with the common people in the streets, had affairs with the daughters of a shoemaker and a farmer, and behaved like a prince of the people rather than the descendant of a divinely inspired dynasty of near superhuman rulers. None of this went down well with the nobility or with his own class, and even the people about to be liberated did not necessarily accept the "Josephine" system. Hungary rose in rebellion, and the Netherlands took the liberation of government for a signal to rise against Austrian rule in general. Nothing could be done to prevent the loss of Belgium and Holland, nor could Emperor Joseph travel into Germany without the permission of his own subject, the King of Prussia. The

crown of the Holy Roman Empire had become the laugh-
ing stock of Europe.

In his private life, Joseph was no luckier than in politics. His first wife, whom he had loved dearly, died
shortly after their marriage, followed by his only child.
He married once again only to find that second marriage
unhappy and frustrating.

He was declared an atheist. His hostility towards the
Church cut off whatever support he could muster from
Pope Pius VI or even from his devoutly religious subjects.
So great was his hatred for the Catholic Church that it
led him to grant complete freedom and equality to all
other religions including the Protestant and Jewish. The
"Edict of Tolerance" was not so much motivated by his
great liberalism as by the thought of hurting the pre-
dominance of the Catholic Church in his lands.

Joseph's other interference in church matters increased the hostility of the Pope. When the Vatican
sent its ambassador to protest against his laws, Joseph
had the ambassador see his minister, Prince Kaunitz. To
emphasize the low state in which the court of Vienna
held the Pope, Prince Kaunitz received the Papal envoy
wearing a dressing gown and pajamas.

Later, to show his good intentions, Joseph invited the
Pope to visit him in Vienna. For centuries no Pope had
traveled outside of Italy, but matters had come to such
a bad impasse between Church and State that Pius VI
accepted the invitation and paid a State visit to Austria.
Afterwards, a communique was issued emphasizing the
friendly nature of the talks between Pope and Emperor,
but what really transpired was somewhat different.

When Pope Pius VI saw that Joseph would not budge
one iota from his intentions to reform the Church as well
as the State, he warned him, "If you continue with these

destructive projects, the hand of God will heavily lie
upon you. An abyss will open before you and, in the best
years of your life, you will sink into it."

Despite the fact that Joseph's police apparatus con-
trolled what was announced to the public, word of the
Papal malediction seeped out. As far as Joseph was concerned, the fact that the Pope had cursed him meant
little. To him, the Pope was merely a political counter-
player. His own religion was science. But the devout
Austrians now turned away from their Emperor, for they
felt that being cursed by the Pope was tantamount to
being blessed by the devil. Resistance against his reforms
grew. His foreign policies failed, and Prussia rose to
even greater power.

In his bitterness the lonely man of Vienna began to
wonder what had caused his downfall. All his good intentions towards freeing his people from age-old abuses
had only aroused their hatred of him. It did not seem
natural that they should react this way. Perhaps the mys-
tic element in the great reformer was not altogether ex-
tinct. In his sleepless night walks he sometimes remarked
to his secretary that "the old man of Rome" had won after
all.

The succession of misfortunes undermined Joseph's
health even though he was still a young man, and he felt
his end was not far off. On January 30, 1790, he decreed
that every one of his laws passed in previous years, all
his reforms, were to be nullified immediately:

"Since we are now convinced that you people prefer
the old ways better than mine and find your happiness
in them, we do not wish to hesitate to give you back that
what you desire."

Within a matter of days he had sought out the Turkish

and French ambassadors and made peace with everyone
with whom he was still in conflict regardless of the necessary concessions. The Hungarian rebels who had complained bitterly that their ancient treasure, the crown
of St. Stephen, was being kept illegally at Vienna, were
suddenly told that the relic would be returned to them
immediately. When the crown arrived back in Hungary,
spontaneous celebration broke out, and it seemed as if
Joseph's imminent removal from the scene would be the
Hungarian's greatest joy. With nothing but bitterness in
his heart and the sure knowledge that he had failed on all
fronts, Joseph passed away less than a month later. He
went through the motions of the last sacraments but assured his priest that he was doing so only as a matter
of record. "Believe me, Father," the Emperor said, "I've
made my peace with God already."

Since Joseph had died childless, the throne now re-
volved to his brother Leopold II. Once again a brilliant
and promising prince ascended the Austrian throne. His
talents, such as they were, were sorely needed. For one
thing Turkey was at war again. Prussia and Poland had
formed an alliance to invade Austria, and Leopold realized that only in making peace with Prussia could he save
his country from invasion. As soon as he had achieved
this peace he returned to the task of rebuilding the absolute empire of his predecessors prior to the reign of his
late brother, Joseph II. Whatever were left of the reforms
undertaken by Joseph were nullified. The French Revolution made him determined to put all his energies to work
in order to prevent any popular uprising, whether in
Austria or elsewhere, for he realized that revolution was
the greatest single threat to all princes regardless of their
nationality.

With his cousins, he planned to liberate King Louis and Queen Marie Antoinette, who were at that time kept prisoners in the Tuileries. To accomplish the rescue, he sent specially trained men to bring the royal couple to neutral soil. As soon as that was accomplished, Leopold was to declare war upon France, not as Archduke of Austria but as head of the Holy Roman Empire and Defender of Christianity against the barbarous and atheistic French revolutionaries.

The plan would have gone well if fate had not intervened. On July 5, 1791, Leopold received word that the King and Queen had been freed and were on their way to the Netherlands. Unexpectedly, however, the plot was foiled. The royal couple, disguised as plain citizens, were riding through the little town of Varennes on their way north when the son of a local postmaster by the name of Drouet recognized them and caused their arrest. They were brought back to Paris and imprisoned.

Despite this blow, Leopold persisted in calling upon the rulers of Christian Europe to unite against the French revolutionaries. But what seemed to be a natural appeal was not heeded by the rulers of Europe, who believed that King Louis would somehow come to terms with the national assembly. The outcome of their refusal is too well known.

About the only positive thing that emerged from Leopold's attempt to rally the princes of Europe against the revolutionaries in France was Prussia's accession to his demands for a lasting peace. On February 28, 1792, a Prussian ambassador arrived in Vienna to prepare for the common war of Prussia and Austria against the French. Leopold was overjoyed. Perhaps he would not be too late to save the lives of his sister and brother-in-law. The day after the arrival of the Prussian ambassador, jubilant at the prospect of positive action in a cause he felt was his destiny to pursue, he rode out to Schönbrunn Castle. That night he was struck down by a mysterious fever and within a matter of hours he was dead.

The Habsburg Empire now fell into the hands of Leopold's nephew Francis. This young man had been brought up at the Imperial court with a view of turning him into a worthy successor to both Joseph and Leopold. However, in a secret report about his student, the boy's educator, Count Colloredo, had written, "The apathy and mental slowness of the Archduke cannot be overcome. No matter what the occasion he just stands there like a piece of wood, his arms and legs awkward, and he would stay in that position to the next day if one wouldn't tell him to move on."

Francis was totally opposed to any form of free thinking, any form of progress, any form of responsibility. He hated his position and was concerned only with his own comforts and rights. He never read books, remarking, "All knowledge endangers my throne."

But it was his lack of knowledge in the area of statecraft that endangered his throne even more. In 1804, he relinquished the German Imperial crown, which no longer had any meaning for the Habsburgs, and assumed instead the title of Emperor Francis I of Austria.

He stood by as the French Emperor Napoleon took Vienna in 1809. If it hadn't been for the military capabilities of his brother, Archduke Charles, the French would have annexed all of Austria to their Empire. As it was, Francis had to sign a humiliating peace with Napoleon and give him his daughter Marie Louise for a wife.

His private life was far from happy. He was married

four times, losing three wives unexpectedly to illness. As the years went on it became clear that the hereditary prince, Ferdinand, who was to succeed Francis was an imbecile. But Francis would not hear of changing the succession to permit a more capable member of the Habsburgs to come to the throne. In an Austria which he had turned into a police state there was no room for open debate of such issues. Consequently, the country looked forward to an uncertain rule when Francis died. This was the more tragic since there were two capable Habsburg princes available—the victor over Napoleon, Archduke Charles, and his brother, Archduke John, a great liberal highly respected and loved by the Austrians.

When Ferdinand succeeded his father in 1835, Europe held its breath. How long would this half-witted, sensitive young man be able to maintain himself on the throne of Austria? For twelve long years Prince Metternich, acting for Ferdinand, managed to keep things under control, but the march of progress could not be held away from Austria's borders forever.

All over Europe revolutions sprang up, and they were sometimes successful. In 1830 a French king had been opposed by the populace. Poland had risen against Russia and been temporarily successful in maintaining her independence. Belgium had broken away from Holland. The old order was dead. The industrialization of Europe and the mounting liberalization of thinking, both among the lower classes and the intellectuals, led to pressure for change. By 1848 this pressure had mounted up to a point where a break was inevitable. That year, revolutions took place not only in Austria, but in France, Italy, Hungary, Bohemia—1848 is synonymous with rebellion.

On December 2, 1848, with Vienna firmly in the hands of the rebels, Emperor Ferdinand, a fugitive in Moravia as guest of the Bishop of Olmütz, signed his abdication.

With the removal of the incompetent ruler, a new era began for the Habsburg Empire. Quite clearly, Ferdinand's incompetence was only the end result of centuries of incest and lack of flexibility on the part of the Habsburgs. On one of those rare occasions when an Austrian ruler did have a natural son to succeed him, that son turned out to be an idiot. Thus, the heavy hand of the curse continued to exert pressure upon the family, and there was really nothing they could do about it. Improvement would mean a total turnabout from the principles the Habsburgs had stood for since the early Middle Ages. But in 1848 they were merely down, not out.

"The revolutionary events of the year 1848 threatened the very existence of the Habsburg empire," wrote Adam Wandruszka. When the eighteen-year-old Francis Joseph was made Emperor, the wags of his time explained the young ruler's reference to himself as "*Wir*," meaning "We," as actually representing the initials of his three generals, for Austria was at that time in the midst of a civil war. Prince Windischgrätz had just liberated Vienna from the rebels. Jellacic was unsuccessfully trying to defeat the Hungarian revolution, while old field marshal Radetzky was doing a lot better in Italy against the insurrection supported by Savoy.

The historian Paul Frischauer characterized the reign of Francis Joseph as dedicated to "the suppression of revolution to remove all resistance to his rule without, however, having any responsibilities himself—those are the guidelines of government for Francis Joseph."

When Hungary refused to accept Francis Joseph as King and instead established a national state under the leadership of the great Hungarian statesman Louis Kossuth, Francis Joseph decided to invade his own province. Since his soldiers were already deeply engaged in Italy and what with the rebels in Austria, he had to accept the military aid of Russia to do so. As a result, two hundred thousand Russian soldiers marched into Hungary, and the Hungarian rebels, who had up to then done well against the Austrians, were overwhelmed. Czar Nicholas turned Hungary back to Francis Joseph, requesting only that the Austrian ruler let bygones be bygones and treat the Hungarians honorably. This, the Emperor promised, but he did not keep his word. Instead, he allowed his military commander, General Julius Haynau, to deal with the rebels as though he were dealing with some foreign province he had just conquered rather than with his own people.

A veritable blood bath followed. Seventeen hundred and sixty-five officers and civilians were sent to prison for long terms, and one hundred fourteen were executed. The members of the national Hungarian government were hanged in effigy in a public square in Budapest. A lady by the name of Baroness Madersbach was publicly whipped for having harbored some freedom fighters, and when her husband learned of it, he committed suicide. All this was, of course, known to the Emperor. Even those among the Austrian politicians who had formerly been in favor of suppressing all rebellion now urged moderation towards Hungary lest all respect of the Hungarian people for their Austrian "brothers" should be forever lost. But Prince Schwarzenberg, the Emperor's first minister, smiled at such a suggestion and replied, "Let's do a bit of hanging instead."

Between 1849 and 1867, Hungary was treated like a conquered province. In various parts of Austria, 258 people were executed during this period. Other revolutionary tribunals sentenced to death many times this number in Hungary alone. Those who criticize the government of Francis Joseph over the death sentences handed out against political rebels rarely mention the deeds of the military tribunals that were not subject to review or supervision by his government. Even so reactionary a politician as the Czar Nicholas I repeatedly warned against executing formerly loyal officers who had surrendered peacefully to the Austrian army, and Prince Metternich, who had retired to Belgium, condemned the executions as unnecessary and against the best interests of the Austrian state. Only the political necessity of coming to terms with what constituted almost one half the territory eventually forced Francis Joseph to reconcile himself with the Hungarians in order to save what was left of his Empire. But for the present, hatred was the order of the day.

It was during the period immediately following the putting down of the Hungarian revolt that the third Habsburg curse originated.

The third curse against the Habsburgs was uttered by the mother of Count Louis Batthyani, one of the Hungarian revolutionaries executed in 1849.

It appears that on August 27, 1849, a counsel of ministers met to divide the rebels into categories according to the severity of their offenses. A letter from General Haynau was read by the minister of justice, Dr. Schmerling, in which the general complained he was being hampered in the suppression of the Hungarian rebellion and in his just execution of the guilty. After much deliberation, General Haynau was given more or less free rein in dealing with the revolutionaries, and thirteen generals were executed on October 6, 1849, bringing the total number of revolutionary leaders who had been executed to nineteen. Among those put to death was the prime minister of the Hungarian freedom government, Count Louis

Batthyani. His mother had submitted a request for an executive pardon to General Haynau, but her plea went unheeded, and her son was executed. It was when word reached her of his death that the third Habsburg curse was pronounced:

"May those responsible for the death of my son never have a happy day again in their lives. May he who ordered this execution be damned forever."

Since General Haynau had been given a free hand to execute the leaders, and since Francis Joseph knew that Batthyani would be executed but did nothing to stop it, surely the curse was meant for him above all others.

Three years after the Hungarian defeat, a former freedom fighter attempted to knife the Emperor. The injury was not serious, and the would-be murderer was hanged immediately. To thank God for the miracle of his escape, Francis Joseph ordered a huge neo-Gothic cathedral to be erected. The building of this church, called the Votive Church, ate up large sums of money which could have been used to better advantage elsewhere in the economically shattered empire. Since the Hungarian attacker had been a tailor by profession, Francis Joseph thereafter refused to have any tailor of any nationality whatsoever fit his clothes on his body. A wooden dummy was fashioned from his measurements, and whenever new uniforms or civilian clothes were needed for the Emperor, his tailors had to work with the dummy alone. The very sight of a tailor was too much for Francis Joseph to bear.

When Russia needed Austrian help during the Crimean War and justly hoped for repayment of the ancient Hungarian debt, Francis Joseph turned a cold shoulder to their pleas and supported their enemies instead. Even his own ministers were aghast at such ingratitude. But Francis Joseph was quite incapable of altruistic feelings for anything that did not benefit himself or the Empire which he thought he alone represented.

In view of Austria's waning position in Germany and her uncertain economic condition, basic prudence alone would have dictated avoidance of any involvement in war or campaigns likely to cost large sums. Only by steering a careful middle course could Austria hope to maintain her position among European nations. But the Emperor would not listen to seasoned professional politicians. Instead, he decided to become his own prime minister and supreme commander of all armies. The actual administration of his armed forces he turned over to his adjutant, Count Gruenne. The Count was one of Francis Joseph's favorite people, a good drinking companion and a fellow who always agreed with his Emperor. That he knew nothing whatsoever about the higher theories of warfare did not disturb the Emperor one bit. Following the adjutant's advice, the Austrian Army was now reduced to learning how to parade properly before the Emperor rather than to engage in complicated strategic maneuvers.

Count Gruenne had great ambitions. Without consulting the foreign minister, Count Buol, he challenged the King of Sardinia to remove his armed forces from the border within three days or else the Austrian Army would take over the little country. When Count Buol learned of what the adjutant had done, he blew his top, for he knew only too well that Sardinia had just concluded a treaty with France under the terms of which France would come to the aid of the Italian kingdom if attacked. All the King of Sardinia had to do was sit still and allow himself to be attacked, and he could be sure of French aid and intervention—and this is precisely what happened. A war had been artificially created. Result—Austria lost Lombardy, one of her richest provinces. The Emperor blamed his generals for having advised him badly, for it never occurred to him that his own deeds were responsible for these defeats.

The heavy hand of fate rested upon Francis Joseph as never before, but he was as yet unaware of it.

The adjutant, Count Gruenne, was dismissed immediately. A number of high-ranking officers were accused of misconduct of the war—innocently, of course, since they had merely been following orders. One of the officers, General von Eynatten, could not bear the idea of a public trial and rather than face the disgrace, hanged himself in his cell. The minister of finance, Baron Bruck, had been summoned by Francis Joseph and accused of mismanagement for not supplying the army with sufficient means regardless of whether he was able to or not. Baron Bruck cut his throat as soon as the Emperor had dismissed him.

But fate had still other misfortunes in store for Francis Joseph. Five years after the Italian debacle, he permitted himself to be drawn into a campaign against Denmark that had nothing to do with the legitimate interests of Austria. He merely sent an expeditionary force to help the Prussians conquer two more provinces, but when it ended successfully, Austria shared in the gains only to lose everything over again when Prince Bismarck managed to talk Francis Joseph out of it a short time later. Thereafter, the Emperor prepared to meet his erstwhile friends, the Prussians, on the battlefield in a desperate attempt to regain Austria's position in Germany proper, but Prussia allied herself with Sardinia, and Austria was caught in the middle. The resulting war was brief and painful. At Königgrätz, in Bohemia, the Austrian Army was cut to pieces with the result that Austria was forbidden any further participation in German affairs. The rest of the Italian possessions, particularly Venice, was forever lost to Austria.

Francis Joseph took this news calmly, but for the first time he did not blame others for Austria's misfortunes. "It seems that I have an unlucky hand," he said. And for the first time some sort of realization that his own bloody deeds had created at least part of the force in operation against him must have entered his consciousness.

At moments like this doubts overcame him, for not all Habsburgs were so steeped in their own traditions that they could not take an objective view of their position. Archduke John, Francis Joseph's uncle and perhaps the best loved of all the Habsburg princes in the nineteenth century, a man who lived among simple people and who had long discarded the ceremonial business of being an archduke, had said some years before, "Perhaps the future of Europe lies in a republic," and he had repeatedly warned Francis Joseph to let the light into his house of government, but to no avail. Incapable of any flexibility, the aging monarch continued on the accursed path that could only lead to ruin for Austria and the Habsburgs.

Things had gotten so bad at court that Empress Elizabeth returned from her far-flung travels to be with her husband in his travails. Because of the chill between them, she had gone on longer and longer trips to foreign countries to try to forget her disappointment with Francis Joseph. But now he needed her, and she felt she could at least try to straighten things out between him and his subjects.

Elizabeth was well liked by everyone in Austria, and it was entirely due to her diplomatic and charming ways that the leader of the Hungarian nobility, Count Julius Andrássy, agreed to high-level discussions with the Emperor. As a result of their meetings, the Austro-Hungarian Empire was born, a dual monarchy in which Hungary and Austria each had separate governments but equal rights and, of course, the same ruler—Francis Joseph. But with the *Ausgleich*, the reconciliation, came a sharp reduction of Francis Joseph's powers. Bitterly realizing that the absolute powers he once held were gradually being taken away from him, he took refuge in hunting and early morning walks, spending more and more of his time outside the capital city of Vienna.

At the same time Francis Joseph had to swallow the bitter pill of a restored Hungary with full powers to run her own affairs, his brother Maximilian allowed himself to be the victim of a political plot hatched by France's Napoleon III. The French Emperor had landed troops in Mexico to make political capital out of the civil war that was then raging between two factions. Napoleon proposed that Maximilian be made Emperor of Mexico. Only a tiny fraction of the Mexicans supported this idea, but Maximilian was so taken with the romantic notion of leading an overseas Empire that he fell in with the plan. "Why, I'll be an Emperor, too," he wrote jubilantly to Francis Joseph. Maximilian and his wife, Charlotte, who was a sister of the Empress of France, landed in Mexico and for a few weeks allowed themselves the luxury of belief in their mission. At the first sign of Mexican resistance, however, the French expeditionary force withdrew, leaving Maximilian to his own resources. Still, he could have saved his life had he been willing to sign the documents of abdication. Too proud to consider that his adventure had been a mistake, he refused and was executed by a firing squad on June 19, 1867. The body was returned to Austria by the country's only naval hero, Admiral William von Tegetthoff, and put to rest in the Habsburg family vault at the Capuchin friars in Vienna. His wife, Charlotte, went mad.

The peculiar aspect of the Habsburg curse that gave so many Habsburg rulers no direct male heir at all, or if there was one, caused great difficulties between father and son, became obvious once again as relations between Crown Prince Rudolph and his father, Francis Joseph, worsened from year to year.

How difficult things were for the liberal Crown Prince can be seen from a report published by Count Carl Lonyay: "Rudolph was a virtual prisoner. He was kept under strict surveillance. No one could visit him unobserved. His correspondence was censored."

When Rudolph's great love, Mary Vetsera, came into his life, they were forced to meet secretly in Rudolph's apartment in the Imperial Palace. Mary was able to gain access to this apartment by means of a secret stairway, and thus the two lovers were able to spend many happy hours together unknown to those who kept Rudolph a virtual prisoner.

Then, on January 28, 1889, Rudolph sent his coachman to bring Mary to his hunting lodge at Mayerling, about an hour's ride outside Vienna. I have previously described the Mayerling tragedy and my private investigation with a well-known psychic in my book *Window to the Past*.

The morning after Mary's arrival at Mayerling, Rudolph

summoned his valet, Loschek, at 6:30 to tell him that he
wished to be awakened again at 7:30 for breakfast. But
when Loschek tried to waken the Crown Prince at the
appointed hour, there was no response to his knock. Feeling something was wrong, he went for help, and returned
with Count Hoyos, a friend of Rudolph. Together, they
broke down the bedroom door and found the young couple in bed. Both had been shot to death.

Several different versions were announced to the
world. At first it was said to have been a hunting accident. Finally, suicide was admitted, but only the Crown
Prince was given an honorable burial. Mary's body was
immediately removed and hidden in a woodshed, where
it lay unattended for two days. Eventually, she was
buried in an unmarked grave after her relatives had been
forced to sign a false document stating that Mary had
committed suicide. By order of the Emperor, all of
Rudolph's documents, even his correspondence were
seized and impounded.

In the cold light of modern research, however, the suicide theory does not hold water. Edward, Prince of
Wales, wrote in a letter to his mother, Queen Victoria,
"Salisbury [the prime minister] is sure that poor Rudolph
and that unfortunate young lady were murdered." Even
the autopsy report available many years later supported
the death by murder rather than by suicide:

"The gun wound of the Crown Prince did not go from
right to left as has been officially declared, and it would
have been natural for suicide, but from left behind the
ear toward the top of the head where the bullet came out
again. Also, other wounds were found on the body. The
revolver that was found next to the bed had not belonged
to the Crown Prince; all six shots had been fired. The shot-

gun wound of the young lady was not found in the temple as had been claimed, but on top of the head. She, too, is said to have had other wounds."

The mystery has not been solved definitely to this day.

To give external expression of his grief, Emperor Francis Joseph immediately ordered the gay hunting lodge turned into a severe Carmelite monastery. (The spot where the two lovers were found dead is now part of the chapel.) The Emperor even disapproved of the way in which his son found death. "He died like a tailor," he is reported to have said. To him, dying like a tailor was about the worst way to leave this earth, for was it not a tailor, after all, and a Hungarian to boot who had attempted to take his life some years before?

But no matter how Francis Joseph felt about the tragedy, there was no gainsaying that the loss of the young heir to the throne meant serious trouble for the Austro-Hungarian Empire. The liberal forces in Austria as well as the nationalists in Hungary had looked towards Rudolph's succession to the throne with renewed hope, and they were willing to wait for a peaceful settlement of their grievances. Now their hope was gone. The old man was back in the saddle, and there was no one on the horizon who could take up the cause of the underdog. Not surprisingly, there had been no advance warning that tragedy was imminent. Although there had been some reported remarks concerning suicide, no one actually thought Rudolph would try to escape life in that manner. This was not because of Church dogma, but because Rudolph's frustrations were as well known to the world as were his ambitions. Rudolph wanted very much to become Emperor. Because of his father's antagonism to-

ward him, Rudolph was sure his suicide would please
the Emperor, and to please the Emperor was the last
thing Rudolph wanted to do.

Evidently, Rudolph had suspected some sort of police
action towards the last days of his life. The Countess
Larisch, who was both Rudolph's cousin and his confi-
dante, had been the only person who knew of Rudolph's
and Mary Vetsera's meetings. In her memoirs, the Countess reports that Rudolph gave her a strongbox to keep for
him. "The Emperor may order my rooms searched at any
moment," the Countess quotes Rudolph as saying. The
Crown Prince instructed her to hand over the strongbox
only to a person offering her the secret code letters R. I.
U. O. The letters had no meaning to the Countess, but she
promised to obey her cousin. After Rudolph's death the
strongbox was indeed picked up by a person offering the
code letters, and that person was Archduke John Salvator.
Every scrap of paper in Rudolph's possession, every bit
of correspondence between himself and his friends or as-
sociates was seized by the secret police of Count Taaffe.
The only thing escaping Taaffe's hands was that strongbox.

IX   Whatever Happened to Archduke John?

On an island outside the city of Gmunden in Austria, connected with the mainland by a wooden bridge, stands the ancient Castle Ort. Built in the tenth century, Ort was burned in 1634 during the peasant wars, and was rebuilt at great expense. Nowadays, the castle itself is not open to tourists; rather they are shown only the courtyard and the cellar. They are, however, told of the unhappy Archduke John Salvator, who once owned it, who disappeared, and who, according to legend, "was never heard from again."

After the archduke's disappearance, the castle changed hands many times as though no one wanted to own it for very long. Finally, in 1869 the deposed Grand Duke Leopold of Tuscany, a member of the Habsburg family bought the entire estate for the sum of 21,000 florins. In order to ensure that he had complete privacy, he ordered the entire area shut off from the rest of the community. The road that passed by the castle was closed. To the north, an artificial canal called the "waiting moat" formed the boundary and was a safe harbor for salt barges during periods of bad weather. During thunderstorms, Lake Traunsee can be very dangerous with high waves that at times give the appearance of an ocean. The "waiting moat" connects with the castle through a narrow path almost hidden by underbrush and trees. Anyone using this path to get to the moat would probably not be noticed from either the town side or the castle itself.

After the death of the Grand Duke of Tuscany, his widow sold the properties into private hands. But in 1878, her son, Archduke John Salvator, felt himself drawn back to the place where he had spent so many happy summers in earlier years, and so returned to the castle.

Hannes Loderbaur in his historical book dealing with Castle Ort points out, however, that sometime before 1890, the archduke broke with his family, laid down all his titles and dignities and assumed a common name, John Ort, and as John Ort, he became a legend in the area.

Archduke John had been jolted from his complacency by the events at Mayerling. Suddenly, he found himself the executor of the political testament of his cousin, Archduke Rudolph, the Crown Prince. He had been given the strongbox to keep, although he did not know what was in it. John Salvator was in a precarious position from that moment on.

To make things worse, he had fallen in love with a totally unsuitable girl, an actress by the name of Margaret Stuebel. It was a case of true love, but even though his mother, Maria Antonia, realized this, she would not consent to a marriage between her son and the actress.

There is a legend in the area around Castle Ort, according to which there once was a giant living and working in the surrounding mountains. Sitting on one of his favorite spots one day, he saw a water nymph bathing naked in the lake below him. The moonlight added a romantic touch to this scene which was repeated night after night, for the nymph was unaware of the giant watching her. This giant, whose name was Erla, fell in love with the little water nymph and decided to marry her. However, he knew that in order to win her, he would have to build her a castle. With the help of his friends, the mountain dwarfs, Erla built an artificial island and then upon that island he built a beautiful castle. When he had finished, though, he found himself in a quandry. How could he, a giant, fit in with the little water nymph. He was much too big for her or she was too small for him. Either way something had to be done about their sizes. In this emergency, he received help from the witch Kranawitha. This friendly witch reduced the giant to human size turning him into a shining knight, and in this guise he entered the castle and married his beloved blond water nymph. But water nymphs live only one summer, and at the end of the year the little blonde passed away. Erla took her body by ship to the middle of the lake and buried her there in the deepest part. To this day, the mountain above that spot is called Erlakogel or Mountain of Erla, and fishermen claim that on full moons one can see a mysterious light at the bottom of the lake. The next day the giant returned to his normal size and used his remaining years to create a giant memorial to his beloved blonde, a mountain called to this day the sleeping nymph.

Whether this is a genuine local legend or one that was inspired by a poem written at the turn of the twentieth century by the poet Josef Steglauer is a moot question. The point is that Dr. Erwin Operschal, the local tourist commissioner, points out a strange parallel between this legend and the love affair between John Salvator and Margaret Stuebel. The giant Erla had to be cut down in size in order to marry his water nymph. Archduke John, the social giant and a member of the Imperial family, had to be reduced to commoner in order to marry his beloved actress. The giant, after marrying the nymph disappears and is never seen again. Archduke John, after marrying the actress, also disappeared and was never seen again. But here the parallel ends.

According to the record, Archduke John, shortly after becoming plain Mr. John Ort and marrying his actress, decided to purchase a ship and sail the seven seas. On a trip to Hamburg he acquired a captain's license and a ship named the *St. Margaretha*. The ship was seaworthy and capable of crossing the ocean to South America, which allegedly was his first goal. His beloved wife was to go along with him on the initial journey. Although there is no proof, John Ort and his wife are said to have gone on board the ship and sailed for South America. The *St. Margaretha* was never heard of again, and it is assumed that the ship with its captain and crew went to the bottom of the sea somewhere in the Straits of Magellan during a storm.

The fact is that neither Archduke John nor the ship was ever heard from again. But we do not really have any objective evidence that *he ever went aboard ship*. The story, it appears, came into being in Austria as a sort of explanation why nothing was heard of the fate of Archduke John. To this day, various antique shops in the area sell what they solemnly swear are the boots of Archduke John or a belt or sword actually once in his possession. According to these antique dealers John Ort must have had a very large wardrobe.

What exactly happened to John Ort?

Mr. Josef Obermayer is a gentle, soft-spoken, slightly built man in his late fifties who currently manages a small roadside inn. In his earlier years he was a salesman, selling many kinds of products and working out of the upper Austrian capital of Linz. These days, however, he is satisfied to live the quiet life of an innkeeper with his wife, with his books and with his unusual interests. These interests have always included psychic phenomena, astrology and alchemy. Mr. Obermayer is a local medium, although he makes no professional pretenses nor does he give "readings" in the traditional sense. But he has a reputation for knowledge not possessed by everyone. As a matter of fact, I was first told about this man by the local inspector of state police, Alois Mayrhuber. It appears that the innkeeper had on several occasions been of use to the police in connection with missing persons and other detective work. It isn't very often that one learns about a local psychic from the police inspector, but, then, Austria is frequently a land of non-conformists and the good inspector of Bad Aussee is a case in point.

I telephoned Mr. Obermayer and explained the purpose of my visit, though I was careful not to give away the exact location of my quest. There was, however, the problem of transportation since I do not drive, and my wife was not able to accompany me. Under the circumstances, Mr. Obermayer suggested that his son, an engineer from Vienna, should drive us to Gmunden.

A few days later, the two Obermayers, Dr. Operschal and I started out for Gmunden. During our drive Mr. Obermayer suddenly remarked that he was aware of a psychic presence, though at the time we were nowhere near Castle Ort.

"I sense a black knight," he said hesitantly. "I see a castle, and this knight is connected with it. I have a feeling someone was killed in there. I don't know who. I see a dead man's head."

For a while he said nothing further. We passed through the little town of Altmünster and drove into a grove of poplar trees. Hidden in the grove was the entrance to the road leading to the lake. As the car emerged from the trees, the long wooden bridge connecting the island and the Castle Ort to the mainland became visible. We left the car at this point and walked across the bridge.

"There is someone dead in that lake," the medium mumbled as we crossed the bridge.

In the sixteenth-century courtyard the official in charge, Forester Senior Grade Johannes Lahrsteiner, waited for us and we entered the cellar. In accordance with my usual practice, I allowed the sensitive a few minutes to acquaint himself with the atmosphere before asking him any questions.

Then I said, "Was any murder committed here?"

The medium nodded.

"Certainly. The black knight with the hood over his face is the one who committed murder. He is still here and wants to be relieved of his guilt feelings."

"Can you tell me if there are any other remnants of the past in this area, any other emotional events you feel?"

"There are five different layers of history in this place," the medium explained. "I sense layers one, two and five, but I can't get the two in between."

We left the cellar, and returned to the courtyard, where Mr. Obermayer remarked, "I get the impression of bad news being received here. A terrible message is being brought here."

Crossing the courtyard, we went to the half of the castle that had been the residence of Archduke John Salvator. The apartment that had once been Archduke John's was now occupied by the local parish priest, and we could not enter it without special permission. While Dr. Operschal busied himself trying to coax the administrator of the castle to let us get into this private apartment, we stood outside waiting.

"Mr. Obermayer," I said, "what sort of end did the one have who once lived in this apartment?"

Without a moment's hesitation, the psychic turned to me and said, "He met a terrible end."

"Did anybody have to leave here under unusual circumstances?"

"I get the feeling of envy. There was something secret known only to those two."

"What two?" I asked.

"John Ort and the unknown one."

"Who was the unknown one?"

"He was his friend and associate."

"What did the two men have in mind?"

Obermayer shook his head. He couldn't supply the answers as quickly.

"How did the man who once lived here die?"

"I get the feeling—in the brook; it may be a river."

"Is he buried in the water?"

"He is not buried there. He was just thrown in."

"Where?"

"I get beid brook."

"Is it far from here? Is the spot on the island or is it outside?"

"Outside. Not here."

On checking the topography of the island later on, I discovered that the so-called "waiting moat," or in German, *wartgraben*, where the salt barges used to wait during storms on the lake, was also known as a *weidgraben*. Could the medium have meant *weid* instead of *beid*?

"Exactly how was he killed? With what weapons?"

"With a dagger."

"Is he tied to this place or has he found rest?"

"He is still here because of old guilt. He, too, has some guilt."

"What kind of guilt?"

"The guilt feelings connect with what he did with the other man. He has been hurt very much. Again, I hear the arrival of bad news has something to do with it."

"Did the terrible news come before he was murdered or after?"

"Before, about two years before he was murdered."

On checking later, I immediately became aware of the elapsed period between the mysterious death of Crown Prince Rudolph on January 20, 1889, and the equally mysterious disappearance of his cousin, Archduke John, exactly two years later.

"Was there any political connection with all this?" I inquired in the apartment.

"Zähler has taken it."

Now the word *Zähler* means counter, or someone who counts, but is also a proper name. I wanted to know what this man had taken. But Obermayer could make neither head nor tail of it. Casually, I asked whether the name Rudolph made any sense to him in this connection.

"You mean Rudolph von Habsburg?"

How the medium picked that name out of any number of Rudolphs is hard to explain logically unless one surmises that he read my thoughts.

"There is a connection. Certain papers exist in the cellar of this building. They have not been found yet."

"In whose handwriting are they?"

"Archduke's."

We quickly walked down into the courtyard and back onto the bridge. Obermayer was visibly shaken. He tried to light a cigarette and asked for matches. When Dr. Operschal handed him his, Mr. Obermayer dropped them. Bending down to pick them up, he looked at me with a startled expression on his face.

"What is it? What is it?" I asked.

"Just now I had a flash. *Thrown out dead.*"

Whatever happened to John Ort? Are his bones somewhere in Lake Traunsee or in the little brook where the salt barges used to wait? Nobody really wants to look for them. The romantic story of his flight to South America and subsequent demise is much more appealing, and it is also a lot better for the tourist business. Henry Lanier assures us in a strange book called *He Did Not Die at Mayerling* that not only did Crown Prince Rudolph and Mary Vetsera not die at Mayerling but escaped to America, but that Archduke John Salvator got away, too, and ended his life happily as a farmer in South America. None of this has any serious evidence to support it, however. Nor has John Salvator's disappearance at sea. Nor has the strongbox Crown Prince Rudolph left in his care ever turned up again. Everyone connected with the case is now dead and gone. But one thing *is* certain: Two of the most able male branches of the ancient Habsburg family tree were cut off in the prime of life, apparently under unexpected and mysterious circumstances.

Both Rudolph and John died young, unexpectedly, and probably violently. The curse was still at work.

X The Beginning of the End

Soon after the death of Crown Prince Rudolph, Francis Ferdinand, the new heir apparent, was sent to Hungary with specific orders to examine the situation carefully but not say anything in public. Even before he was made the official heir, Francis Ferdinand was already prevented from being himself. The relationship between Emperor Francis Joseph and the young man started out on the wrong foot, and it appeared that he was being treated even worse now than while Rudolph was still alive. Puzzled by this strange attitude on the part of the Emperor, Francis Ferdinand remarked, "It looks as if I were at fault in the Mayerling affair. It appears my face brings back unhappy memories."

Not only were the two men politically miles apart; they hated each other personally as well. When Francis Ferdinand fell in love with the Countess Chotek, the aging Emperor insisted that should he marry the Countess, she could never be Empress nor could their children have any rights whatsoever in the succession to the throne. Even though Countess Chotek came from an ancient and noble Bohemian family, it wasn't good enough for Emperor Francis Joseph who had personally revised the family laws some years previously. The impasse persisted. Even Empress Elizabeth, who had returned specially from one of her many journeys abroad to intervene with her husband on behalf of the Crown Prince, failed to move the Emperor one inch. Francis Ferdinand had to take a solemn oath depriving his future wife and their children of all rights to the succession. If anything, this "inhuman" treatment made him hate the man he was to succeed even more. But the curse of the Habsburgs didn't always hit home swiftly and suddenly. In some instances, it appears, it worked its way up slowly to the character of a man until it had hollowed out all there was left of his humanity. In the case of Francis Joseph this took a lifetime, but in the end the curse was triumphant. Very little emotion remained in the aging monarch.

Empress Elizabeth left again, disappointed by her husband's inflexibility. On September 10, 1889, she found herself in Geneva, trying to be inconspicuous and enjoying what little there was to be enjoyed for someone in her position and possessed with her strong leanings towards melancholia. All over Europe the anarchist movement was seething with activity. The murder of a prominent member of the ruling class was a symbolic expression of their disdain for the system, whether or not that member had anything to do directly with their political aims. Thus, the beautiful and innocent person of Empress Elizabeth seemed like a good target for an anarchist attack. One morning as she was waiting to board a steamer on Lake Geneva, a young anarchist stepped forward and knifed her to death. All Europe was shocked at the suddenness of the attack, the tragic news that had struck the House of Austria once again. But Francis Joseph received the terrible word without flexing a muscle of his face.

His only comment was, "It appears I'm not being spared anything."

As the years went by and the twentieth century dawned, Francis Joseph became less and less aware of the political realities of his day. It is said that the news of German support for his side in any common conflict with the western powers filled him with disdain. "Go ahead and beat those Prussians," he is said to have remarked as if the Battle of Königgrätz and the year 1866 were still fresh in his mind. But history decreed otherwise. The more his many nationalities demanded independence and rights, the more he shut himself away from them, letting his ministers and officials deal with the problems at hand. He was seventy-seven years of age when he was forced to sign a new constitution guaranteeing free and equal voting rights to one and all in his Empire.

Only a year after this, acting on bad advice, he ordered two formerly Turkish provinces, Bosnia and Herzegovina, occupied by Austrian troops regardless of the desire of their populations. This brought Austria even deeper into the Balkans, closer to Russia and into areas where she really had no business. It also stirred up the resistance of Serbia and other small nations in the area. When Crown Prince Francis Ferdinand and his wife, by now known as the Duchess of Hohenberg, visited the city of Sarajevo in Yugoslavia, they became the victims of an attack. The Serbian conspirators not only snuffed out the lives of Austria's Crown Prince and his wife, but also started World War I. Soon after the terrible news had been received by the aging Emperor, it became clear that some sort of action was called for to show that Austria would not take such an insult without retaliation. Meanwhile, the funeral procession arrived at the western railroad station in Vienna. However, because the Duchess of Hohenberg was not, after all, of Imperial blood, she could not be given the royal funeral. Francis Joseph saw to that. Under the circumstances, the two coffins were given a simple cortege in the hope that the procession would not attract too many of the elite. But to everyone's surprise there appeared a group of dignified men in black who insisted on joining the cortege. These men were members of Austria's high aristocracy, and their presence in the funeral procession was a silent and dignified protest against the Emperor's inhuman treatment of his successor, even in death.

But the moment of truth was close at hand. The commander-in-chief, Conrad von Hötzendorf, assured himself of German support and then asked the Emperor if he should attack Serbia. The awful truth is that the future of Europe lay in the hands of an eighty-four-year-old man who was filled with prejudices and perhaps no longer entirely in full possession of his mental powers. Should Austria attack Serbia if the Germans were with her? "In that case, yes," was the Emperor's reply, and World War I with its millions of dead, the result. Having made his decision, he withdrew to his villa at Ischl.

The heir to the throne now was Archduke Charles, Francis Joseph's great-nephew, who had married the right kind of woman, had children galore and, all in all, was a nice young man who was not likely to cause any problems.

Because Francis Joseph had been such a stone-faced monument in his later years, never showing any emotions, never letting anyone in on his inner feelings, I wondered whether some of his innermost thoughts might not be preserved in the atmosphere of the place where he

spent so much time during his last years. That place was
Schönbrunn Palace, since the aging and ailing Emperor
preferred the sprawling, majestic appointments of Schönbrunn to the forbidding, somber, high-ceilinged rooms
of the Imperial Palace in the city. At Schönbrunn he
could go out into the park, walk in his private rose garden
where no one could observe him since the gardeners had
seen to it that the bushes hid him from view. Here he also
died.

But in keeping with his honest desire to be unpreten-
tious, to present the picture of a first servant of the state
to the world, he lived in comparatively modest quarters
even in so magnificent a palace as Schönbrunn. Part of
the second story in the right wing was set aside as the
Imperial apartment. One enters across the wide courtyard and turns right, goes up the magnificent marble
stairs to the second story and there enters the apartment
itself. There is a large reception room where dignitaries
and anyone wishing to see the Emperor would wait, for
Francis Joseph saw a great many people even in his later
years when a constitutional government had already become reality. He still liked to conduct many affairs of
State in person. Thus, there was a continual coming and
going of people, and the overflow had to wait in this reception room. From the reception room one enters the
office of the Emperor, a very large room situated in the
corner and overlooking the inner courtyard. Although
the other rooms in the palace are exquisitely furnished in
rococo, the office differs in contrast in that the Emperor's
simple, wooden desk is functional. From the office one
turns the corner and walks straight into the royal bedroom. Again, this is a large room, and the simple, iron
soldier's bed he used throughout his life, the bed in which
he died, stands in one corner. Until the end, Francis Jo-

seph did not use running water to wash with. He insisted
on the primitive arrangements of a washstand with
pitcher and basin.

Getting into the private apartment of the Emperor was
not easy, but going there at a time when no tourists were
about was even harder to manage. Nevertheless, with the
help of the Austrian tourist authorities and the Vienna
Tourist Committee, I was able to arrange for myself and
two friends to visit after hours so that we could have a
quiet moment of meditation in the rooms I considered
most likely to have an imprint from the past. The official
tours end at nine o'clock, and promptly at that hour we
were let into the private apartment and told we had exactly one hour before we had to leave unless we wanted
to be locked in for the night.

With me were two old friends, both of them psychic,
and Dr. Elizabeth Zauhbauer of the Austrian Tourist
Service. My two psychic friends were Mrs. Edith Riedl,
a venerable lady of Vienna society, who had served as my
medium on many previous occasions, and Mrs. Hertha
Fischer, a physical therapist by profession, who has had
ESP experiences all her life.

While the two ladies were trying to get some sort of
psychic impression, I took a number of photographs in
the dimly lit rooms. One of these photographs clearly
shows a manifestation of sorts—an amorphous figure—between two of the chairs in Francis Joseph's bedroom.

After we walked from the office into the bedroom, I
questioned my friends as to any impressions they might
be receiving. Mrs. Riedl had been at Schönbrunn before
since her father had lived here in the times of Emperor
Francis Joseph. Thus, she was familiar with the details
of the apartment beyond anything a tourist guide would

know. In fact, she knew the position of furniture that
had been moved since the end of the Empire. She immediately pointed out that a basin was missing from the
bedroom. This was a small basin which the Emperor used
when he was bathed by his valet.

"The first man I ever saw in death was Emperor
Francis Joseph," Mrs. Riedl explained. "I was very young
at the time, but I remember distinctly seeing the Emperor
on his bed covered with a piece of muslin and a few roses
strewn upon it. At the foot of the bed kneeled Katharina
Schratt (his companion in his later years). At that moment the wife of the next Emperor, Charles, Empress Zita
entered the room and without a word, Mrs. Schratt rose
and left."

At the time of the Emperor's death, Mrs. Riedl was
seventeen years old. Her father was one of the high officials of the Emperor's own chancellery. After the death,
her father turned to her and said sadly, "Now everything
is finished for us."

On the day before his death, the Emperor had insisted
on his usual routine of seeing people and signing documents. As the Emperor signed one paper after another,
his hand slowed down. At his right side stood Mrs.
Riedl's father, as he had stood for many years. Although
he did not dare suggest that he might help the Emperor
with the signatures, Francis Joseph somehow knew what
his faithful aide was thinking. Looking up at him, he said,
"*Herr Hofrat*, please help me with this." So it happened
that the last signature put on any document on earth by
the dying Emperor was written with a hand led cau-
tiously by Mrs. Riedl's father.

Encouraged by this gesture of reliance upon him, Mrs.
Riedl's father then suggested, "Your majesty should rest
now," something no one in his position would have dared

say under ordinary circumstances. To his surprise, however, the Emperor smiled wryly and replied, "I will be resting soon enough."

Less than twenty-four hours later Francis Joseph was gone.

"Do you feel anything in the atmosphere of this room beyond what the ordinary senses can grasp?" I asked Mrs. Riedl.

"I think if Francis Joseph would be drawn back to his former home, he would have preferred Ischl rather than this place where he was never happy. But I sense the presence of Katharina Schratt here. She was here often in life."

"What feeling do you have concerning any unfinished business around here? Do you feel anything in the atmosphere?"

"I get the feeling that the old Emperor asks himself, 'What could I have done better?' "

"What about the murder of Empress Elizabeth? Did that not disturb him greatly?"

"Let me tell you something about that murder," Mrs. Riedl replied excitedly. "This is not generally known nor has it been published as far as I know, but my father told me of this, at the time asking me not to talk about it. But so much time has gone by I see no reason why I shouldn't tell you.

"When Empress Elizabeth traveled abroad she had with her a number of people, among them a lady-in-waiting who never left her side. That fateful day the lady-in-waiting was the target of the murderer, not the Empress. The murderer had decided to make an example of her since he considered her one of his own people who had no business serving the Habsburgs. His knife was poised to hit the lady-in-waiting when suddenly the Empress dashed ahead of her lady and received the mortal wound instead."

"But why was this version never heard publicly?"

"What good would it have done?"

Could it be that the martyrdom of the beloved and beautiful Empress at the hands of the hated anarchist made better political capital than the accidental knifing of the Empress with a lowly lady-in-waiting as the real target? Or was the curse hitting at Francis Joseph through his wife even though she was not born a Habsburg?

Either way, the murder fitted in well with the pattern of unexpected and extraordinary misfortunes that had befallen the Habsburg family and that continued to occur evidently without the Habsburgs being able to do anything about them.

Throughout his eighty-six years of life, Francis Joseph was aware of the essentially pessimistic qualities of his ways. Frequently, he would remark that he was standing on a lost position, but he had to fight to the last breath to save his honor and that he expected to go down eventually but with his honors intact. Years before his death he had an uncanny feeling of impending catastrophe. In his last will and testament he wrote, "In the event that the crown should not remain with our family, I desire that my daughter Gisela should take her share of the fortune with her and invest it in Germany where it is safer than in Vienna." Was the Emperor suggesting to his daughter that she might be safer in another country, safe from the long hand of the Habsburg curse?

Very few members of the family escaped it entirely. His granddaughter, Elizabeth, the only child of ill-fated

Rudolph, had managed it by marrying a socialist politician, Leopold Petznek. In doing so, she shed the name
of Habsburg, of course, as well as severing all links with
her family, but she survived and led a happy bourgeois
existence.

In 1848, when Emperor Ferdinand was told that the
rebels were storming the Imperial palace, he turned to
his ministers and asked, "Why, do they have *permission*
to do that?" From those naïve days through a long chain
of personal and national misfortunes beyond that which
one could naturally expect in the course of history,
Francis Joseph arrived at a far more somber and realistic
appraisal of his own position: "I'm not being spared *anything.*" Even his death could not put the curse to rest.
There was still a Habsburg Empire even if it was an em-
battled one. The last act was yet to come.

In those stormy, chilly days after the body of the only
Emperor most living Austrians ever knew had left Schönbrunn Palace, few if any of his subjects gave thought to
an ancient curse. Through the years, birds had congre-
gated around Schönbrunn as they had in earlier centuries
in the yards of the palace in the inner city when the area
was still relatively open. Among those birds, blackbirds
were prominent. True, they were not hawks, but, then,
hawks are not native to Vienna.

Shortly after Francis Joseph died, the blackbirds
thinned out around the palace, though no one seemed
to know why. Only a handful remained, even though
blackbirds don't mind the cold Austrian winters. Francis
Joseph's successor, Charles, did not reside at Schönbrunn.
His modest nature felt ill at ease in so magnificent a place,

and besides, the war required his continuous presence near the front lines.

Two years later, when the Habsburg Empire fell altogether, the last blackbirds disappeared from Schönbrunn. There hasn't been one in the park since.

Now it's a long way from the hawks of the twelfth century to the blackbirds of the twentieth. Similar dire predictions about the birds leaving the "sinking ship" of royalty have been related concerning the Tower of London, its ravens and the English royal family. At this writing, the Tower ravens are still there.

The original curse, according to my late historian-friend J., called upon "the birds" as witnesses. In those distant days, hawks were quite commonplace. They are no longer so in this century. The common bird is now the blackbird, just as symbolic of tragedy because of its color. Hawks or blackbirds—the fact *is* that substantial numbers of blackbirds disappeared practically overnight from Schönbrunn when the end came.

There is nothing logical in their disappearance; nothing that could account for it. Only the tradition of the Habsburg curse.

XI Dissolution of an Empire:
Has the Curse Run Its Course?

Charles I was twenty-nine years of age when he succeeded his great-uncle. It was much too late to do anything constructive about the disaster that was about to befall the Austro-Hungarian Empire. His attempt to conclude a separate peace failed. His suggestions to turn Austria belatedly into a multi-national state met with resistance from the nationalities themselves who already had other plans. They no longer wanted to be part of any Empire but wished to go their own separate ways. Everyone felt defeat in the air, and it was only a matter of time before it became objective reality.

Meanwhile, his ministers tried to conclude peace with the allies and save what could be saved, which wasn't very much.

In November 1918 Karl Werkmann, the last secretary of the Imperial government, advised Charles that everything had fallen apart. Under the circumstances, he signed a manifesto prepared for him by his ministers:

"Since my accession to the throne, I have tried incessantly to lead my people out of the horrors of war, a war I am not guilty of. I did not hesitate to restore the constitutional life and have shown the people the road to in-

dependent development. Now the people have taken
over the government through their representatives. I re-
sign all participation in matters of State. *Only peace
within* can heal the wounds of this war."

Of all the Habsburg rulers Charles was certainly the
most peaceful and the one most sincerely devoted to
avoiding future conflicts. Unfortunately, he was unable to
do much about his aims in his lifetime.

Charles considered his resignation more of a relief than
the workings of an old curse. Even though his wife, the
ambitious Empress Zita, tried to change his mind about
signing the declaration, he insisted, feeling that remov-
ing himself from office was a step towards the "inner
peace" he held vital for the future of his beloved
country.

Under the circumstances, his staying at Schönbrunn
would have been preposterous. What he needed was a
small, quiet residence somewhere in the countryside. It
so happened that fifty kilometers east of Vienna there
stood a modest hunting lodge called Eckartsau, a far cry
from the luxurious appointments at Schönbrunn. Eckartsau was just the place to move with his family. Unfortunately, the house was far from ready to receive the
Imperial family. Furniture was sparse, and they had to
manage as best they could. Almost their sole protection
was an English officer sent by King George V, a certain
Lieutenant Colonel E. L. Strutt whose job it was to prevent violence being done to the former Austrian Emperor.

But the stay at Eckartsau, so close to the spot where
the first Habsburg Emperor Rudolph had decisively defeated Bohemia's King Ottocar, was a short one. The
provisional government of the republic was not satisfied
to have a former Emperor and his family live among other

citizens. In a stormy session on November 12, 1918, it was decided that Charles had to forfeit his throne and leave the country with his family. At the same time, the entire property of the dynasty Habsburg-Lorraine was to be seized and become property of the State. The national assembly had to pass on the validity of this horrendous law. But Charles did not wish to wait for fate to strike him the final blow. He realized that it was time to leave.

On March 23, 1919, Charles and his family left Austria on a special train, the last symbol of majesty he had been able to wring from his successor government. With him went a few hand-picked friends and servants. At first the Imperial family went to Castle Wartegg near Lake Constance, a house belonging to a relative of the Empress, but the house proved to be too small, so the family moved to Villa Pragins on Lake Geneva instead. Meanwhile, they learned the full impact of the so-called Habsburg law. All members of the family, whether directly connected with the ruling line or not, had to leave Austria unless they would foreswear their membership in the family itself and surrender their names and titles. In fact, the use of any titles of nobility or special preferential addresses was strictly forbidden. Even purely private properties of members of the Habsburg family were seized under the pretext that they belonged to the same family whence the ruling house had come. Later on this law was changed and eventually repealed. But the impact of its original disclosure hit Charles very hard. How could a country which had been tied to his family for seven hundred years act so cruelly in the end?

Two years after the former Emperor had entered Switzerland, he allowed himself to be convinced that Hungary, if not Austria, wanted him back. Somehow the Hungarians were more likely to welcome a monarchy than the socialistically inclined Austrians. Charles took an ordinary train from Switzerland to Vienna. On March 25, 1921, he went unannounced and unrecognized to the apartment of a friend of his youth, Count von Erdoedy. The following morning they drove to the Hungarian border in a taxicab. Without being challenged, the two men continued onto Hungarian soil and spent the night at the palace of the Bishop of Szombathely. In Budapest they were cordially received by Admiral Horthy. The admiral had just defeated a Communist government and was now officially the regent of the kingdom of Hungary. Charles was just thinking that better times were at hand when word reached him that the newly created state of Czechoslovakia would consider his restoration a case of war. Under the circumstances, Admiral Horthy could not turn the reins of government over to Charles, and the ex-Emperor returned to Switzerland.

As though he had not had enough troubles already, the fact that he had used his political asylum in Switzerland for activities of this nature caused the provincial government to withdraw his permit of residence. He moved to another province of Switzerland not far from where the remnants of the castle New Habsburg stand above Lake Lucerne. Although the castle New Habsburg relates to a sideline of the ruling house, a sentimental tie existed between it and the distant cousins in Austria.

Charles was pursuing his idea of a United States of Austria, which would include Austria, Hungary, Czechoslovakia, Rumania and Yugoslavia, regardless of their form of government. With things looking up, his Hungarian friends decided the chances of success for his plan were better, and they insisted Charles return to Hungary. On October 20, Charles and Zita flew to Hungary and drove to the town of Ödenburg. He had not undertaken this daring trip without some help from his allies. In France, for instance, the possibility of a union between Austria and Germany was eyed suspiciously, but Charles's plan for a Danubian federation seemed to promise a counterbalance.

From Ödenburg, the couple drove towards Budapest with one battalion of royal troops. But on the way the regent, Admiral Horthy, intercepted the group and in order to avoid any bloodshed, Charles withdrew. He took residence in the old Benedictine Abbey Tihany on the shore of Lake Balaton, and there the Hungarian government tried in vain to make him sign a declaration of resignation. Charles, however, steadfastly refused to give up the Hungarian throne even though fate had dealt him one blow after another apparently without cause. The Hungarian government therefore declared him and his house without further rights in Hungary.

Once again the English government took matters in hand. A gunboat called the *Glow Worm* was sent to Hungary. Charles and Zita were put aboard ship and slowly transported down the Danube through Hungary, Rumania and down to the Black Sea where the cruiser *Cardiff* took them aboard. Nobody knew where they were going. Only during the last few days before their arrival at Madeira, an island belonging to Portugal, were the Imperial couple informed of their new place of exile.

It reminded Charles of the fate of Napoleon.

Charles was without any means now, but a local banker offered him his summer house situated high in the mountains as a residence. This was a gesture of kindness, but once again fate made something else of it. The house was ideal during the hot summer months because of its location, but on February 18, the day of Charles and Zita's arrival, the mountain top was damp, and Charles fell ill shortly after his arrival. His lungs could not withstand the sudden change from one climate to another, and it soon became clear that he had very little time left on earth. On April 1, 1922, two months after the onslaught of his illness, Charles I, last ruling Emperor of the House of Habsburg, died and was buried in a little Portuguese church on a mountain top of Madeira. His body rests in a simple metal coffin, and on it there is a crown of thorns and the inscription, "Thy will be done."

With the death of the last ruling Habsburg, the family ceased to be of importance in Europe. All members were banished from Austria proper and lived scattered throughout the world. If any Habsburg prince had stepped on Austrian soil, he would have been arrested immediately. Most of the Habsburg properties now belong to the State with the exception of some minor estates belonging to secondary branches of the family. To this day, the Imperial villa of Ischl is in private hands. Emperor Charles, his widow Zita, and his sons and daughters are known primarily to a handful of admirers and Austrians scattered throughout the world who chose to remain loyal to the dynasty, sometimes for romantic rather than for political reasons.

Since there were no more ruling Habsburgs, it is difficult to ascertain whether the curse had finally ceased and the original vow fulfilled. Of all the Habsburg rulers, only the last one, Charles, was almost totally free from guilt and, cut off in the prime of life, might conceivably have taken across the eternal threshold some unused energies capable of being tapped through psychic means.

In late spring of 1955 I appeared on Pittsburgh television and radio. Among those who caught my appearance was a schoolteacher from nearby Industry, Pennsylvania, by the name of Marianne Elko. Mrs. Elko wrote to me in German out of fear that a letter in English might fall into the wrong hands. As a schoolteacher, she was well aware of the prejudices held by some school boards against psychics. As a result of the amazing predictions Mrs. Elko had made before witnesses concerning the death of President Kennedy and his brother and of many lesser people—all of which were checked out and found to be accurate—I investigated her claim and interviewed her in Pittsburgh. It was clear to me that she had no ulterior motives in disclosing the information and that her sole interest was in serving in whatever capacity she was able. Since then she has spoken of her mediumistic experiences before small groups, has given sample readings and, in general, been quietly but effectively active as a semi-professional medium despite the fact that the school board still isn't crazy about it. But she is a very good art teacher and somehow has managed to maintain both careers.

Apparently, a number of deceased individuals come to her when she is asleep as well as when she is awake. They bring messages for the living, all with urgent requests to be transmitted to individuals of whom she has no knowledge. The most startling of these visitors was the late Emperor Charles of Austria who "came to her" in April of 1962, identified himself properly and requested that she transmit a certain message from him to an old friend of his in Vienna.

"When was the first time you had contact with Emperor Charles I of Austria?"

"It was the first of April, 1962. He mentioned it was the fortieth anniversary of his death."

"How did he come to you?"

"Clairvoyantly. All of a sudden I felt an urgency of grabbing a piece of paper to write."

"Had you any interest in this man for any reason?"

"No interest whatsoever."

"What was the message?"

"He told me the world was heading for disaster. And then he gave me the address of a Dr. Arthur Werner, Vienna 6. He told me to write to Dr. Werner and tell him he is working on the salvation of the world. I said, I will make a fool out of myself writing to him, and he said no you will not because he will *recognize the message as coming from me*. So I wrote to this Dr. Werner of whom I had never heard, and he wrote back all right. He was very much surprised. But he admitted that he had been a good friend of Emperor Charles."

"Anything else?"

"Charles also wanted me to tell his son that at least some of the family would resettle in Austria, but his son Otto would stay in Munich."

"Did you see him or hear him?"

"I saw him clairvoyantly. He had on a trench coat; he looked in his early forties, and he had the collar up, and a hat on. The hat was darker than the coat; it was a sports hat. He introduced himself as 'Karl of Austria.' He also spoke of *a terrible destruction in 1988*. There is only a short time left for a change of direction. There will be a war. It will hit America badly. Europe will be less hurt. A two-bomb war, thermophysical and germ warfare. A germ like the Asian flu. He called it C_3."

"When was the next time you heard from him?"

"In 1966, when I was in Regensburg, Germany, and passed a newsstand. I read an article about the Habsburgs coming home. I saw the paper, then walked away, and then I saw him standing there, *actually standing in the doorway* of the old city gate. Then, on January 26, 1972, he spoke to me in the kitchen at home. He complained that he was not interested in *becoming a saint.*"

"Did you know at the time that anyone was trying to make him a saint?"*

"No. He made me draw a pattern, giving me the names of all his friends and when they died. If you connect the dates, it becomes a drawing."

"Who were these friends?"

"They are in an organization which keeps up his memory."

"Do you remember the names?"

"No, I have no recollection. But I wrote it out once and sent it to Dr. Werner."

"In other words, if you connect the points representing the various friends supporting him, if you make lines between them it becomes an iron cross. What is the significance of that?"

"The significance is that the group used this symbol. He showed me one more pattern with twelve parts to the circle. Kennedy died at the "11" and Pope John died in June, that is the "six," and he himself died in April, that is the "four." Connect these points, and you get a picture of *praying hands*. He wanted this used on two sides of a medal. There would be some protection in it, like a talisman."

* According to Arthur Werner, *"Otto von Habsburg,"* p. 95, there was in July 1949 a movement towards the beatification of "Charles of Austria, Servant of God." The first phase of this process, the so-called episcopal process of information, was completed in the archbishopric of Vienna on the thirty-second anniversary of the death of the late Emperor, April 1, 1954. The case was then forwarded to the Vatican for further action.

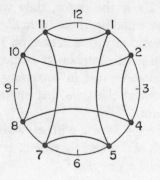

"Was there some form of curse on the family?"

"In the thirteenth century there was . . . I see a young girl, and she was not allowed to get married and was murdered. She had dark brown hair, an outstanding beauty, but she was a commoner. I see her strangled. A very tall, dark man strangled her. It was a thirteenth-century castle, *high up*, and without windows, overlooking a small river. I see it at the foothills of the Alps, but not on a high mountain, on a hill."

"Who pronounced this curse?"

"I think it was a woman. She was only nineteen. She

cursed them in the line of succession. She cursed them not to have sons, or something like that. Something that she thought would hurt them very deeply. She wished them sickness, especially in childbearing. She had a white dress on; could she have been in prison?"

"Which events were due to that curse?"

"A very bloody battle, in the fifteenth century, between mountains . . . broken lances . . . a shield with a cross on it, a red cross. And I see one man with a wound on his neck, dying."

There are several points of interest in Mrs. Elko's testimony, though why a man like Charles of Austria should come through an obscure Pennsylvania art teacher is puzzling. Perhaps he needed a simple vehicle, someone who did not know anything about him and someone who would have no interest in exploiting his communications, either. That a man who is forced to conclude a disastrous war in which millions are killed would try to make up for his accumulated guilt is also understandable. From the very first, Charles I had protested against war even at the time when he was supposed to be leading his army to victory. Thus, the position, post mortem, that he and other distinguished souls on the other side of the veil could influence mankind so that the final destruction would not take place is not only believable but completely in line with the characters of those involved.

On an objective and scientific basis, only the matter of his contact with Dr. Arthur Werner remained to be investigated. If what Mrs. Elko claimed was true, then it constituted valuable evidence for the continued existence of Emperor Charles on the other side of life.

On August 3, 1971, I sat across a laden desk from Dr.

Arthur Werner in Vienna. The amazing thing was that a letter addressed by Mrs. Elko merely to Dr. Arthur Werner, Vienna 6, had actually been delivered to him! Dr. Werner works primarily as a research consultant and magazine publisher in a number of fields. His avocation is being a Habsburg expert, and he has written several books dealing with the Habsburg family, notably his biography of Otto von Habsburg.

I asked Dr. Werner whether he remembered receiving a letter from Mrs. Elko.

"Oh yes," he said. "That was quite a surprise. I didn't know this lady, and all of a sudden I received this letter. I have no idea how she found out about me."

"Is there any way in which she could have learned of your good relationship with the Habsburgs, especially the Emperor Charles?" I asked.

Dr. Werner shook his head. "I doubt it very much."

"Do you accept the evidence that this message received by Mrs. Elko is really from the late Emperor Charles of Austria?"

Dr. Werner scratched his ear and looked somewhat perplexed.

"It looks that way, doesn't it?" he finally replied with a smile.

With the end of the Habsburg dynasty in Austria, the family became merely a distinguished group of refugees living in various parts of the world. The tradition, of course, was kept up, especially as Zita, the ambitious widow of Emperor Charles insisted on strict adherence to the Habsburg family laws and aspirations. Otto became not only heir apparent, but was actually made Emperor of Austria by acclamation. To his followers and friends he is "The Emperor."

Otto, however, harbors no such lofty ambitions. A studious man, he has earned a doctorate in politics and social science and is the author of a number of publications dealing primarily with the one burning wish in his heart: to unite Europe in a supernational state. Thus, the ancient desire of the Habsburgs to unite Europe into an Empire called the Holy Roman Empire has come full circle with one important exception. The Europe Otto von Habsburg wants to see rise from the multi-national jigsaw puzzle it now represents is a continent without hatred and without political boundaries. Above all, it is a state in which no single family is paramount. Perhaps there is within Otto an unconscious desire to atone for the past wrongs his predecessors have brought on Europe. During World War II he was instrumental in preventing Austria's being divided into an American and a Russian zone, thus forestalling a fate similar to Korea or Vietnam. His brothers and sisters—there were eight children in this family—have all been active in social services or refugee service or some other form of humanitarian pursuits. Despite the fact that the Habsburgs, until recently, were not permitted to return to their former homeland, or even to spend brief visits there, the family never gave up hope that they might some day be able to return and continue a close relationship with Austria, which even the republican government had finally to acknowledge. Many members were permitted to return to Austria and live there peacefully. The only restriction concerns the use of the title. The name Habsburg-Lorraine was all right so long as they did not call themselves princes or archdukes publicly. But in title-conscious Austria, such a law will never stick. To the average Austrian, unless he is a dyed-in-the-wool socialist, anyone who is well dressed is automatically a baron or at least *"Herr Doc-*

tor." No Habsburg has as yet been prosecuted for being
called an archduke or a count. In the Vienna telephone
directory alone there are six or seven Habsburg-
Lorraines. None of these are descendants of the Imperial
line, but nevertheless, they are cousins of the ruling
house. Otto himself has not been able to return to Vienna,
but that is only a matter of time. He lives in a sprawling
house near Lake Staremberg just over the border in
Bavaria. His sister Adelaid lives with him. His staff is
small. Whether there is anything to the fabulous Habsburg fortune amassed by Empress Maria Theresa in the
eighteenth century and hidden away somewhere towards
a possible emergency, no one can tell for sure. But Otto's
style of living certainly does not show extreme wealth.

The new Habsburg program as emphasized in Otto's
booklet "Austria and the Europe of Tomorrow" envisions
such amazing things as complete freedom of choice of
residence, complete freedom of choice of employment,
education, the right to build, the right to move capital
freely, the creation of an all-European citizenship, of a
single currency for all Europe, the pooling of all economic resources world-wide, and the total divestment of
national sovereignty. Otto's plan would create a Europe
of four hundred million people to become the fourth
world power. He sees this as a counter-balance to American, Russian and Chinese pressure. But not once in his
numerous public appearances has Otto touched upon the
question of his succession to the Austrian throne. There
is no doubt about it: Neither he nor his brothers or sisters
have the slightest interest in returning to the position
of the ruling dynasty in either Austria or Hungary but
only to be involved in the creation of a European state.

With so much positive action being employed by the
living members of the Habsburg dynasty, one wonders

whether the ancient curse may not have been blunted after all. As far as the former ruling line of the House of Habsburg is concerned, there do not seem to be any misfortunes recorded except that of banishment. Only the head of the house, Otto, has not been able to return to his homeland, but he has made no serious attempt to do so.

The subject of a Habsburg curse was never a popular one in Austria while the Habsburgs were in power and of little impact after they were no longer of consequence. Even so experienced a researcher as Dr. Hans Leo Mikoletzy, the head of the Austrian State Archives, had never heard of such a curse, but he referred me to an old historical volume containing traditions and legends about Austria. That book, which he called the work of Banduzzi, could not be located either at first glance. When the work was finally found, it turned out to be authored by a certain Ponduzzi. Dr. Maria Meyer of the State Archives was kind enough to go through it with the hope of finding some reference to the mysterious curse, but there was nothing in print. On a visit to the former Imperial villa Ischl, I mentioned my quest to the administrator of the villa, Count Kinsky. He suggested I contact a friend of his who was familiar with the Habsburg traditions, Prince Clary, of an ancient Austrian family originally of French origin, who lives in Venice. He, too, had never heard of the Habsburg curse and doubted that it existed:

"That does not mean that I do not believe it exists. Quite to the contrary, I believe it possible for a building, or a person, or even an entire family to be struck by a curse. You know the history of the island Lacrona, in Dalmatia, or the curse leveled against the French family

La Tremoille, or perhaps the one uttered by a Polish priest during the Polish parliament of 1773 against three specific families . . . the Habsburgs were mostly happy people. John the Murderer was an exception. The history of the Habsburgs is otherwise free of murder and cruelty which were so common in other royal families. Certainly, Francis Joseph was struck by misfortune, but one mustn't forget that he was a young man when he took over during the revolutionary year, 1848. Despite reverses and two lost wars, he managed, thanks to his great ability as a ruler, to maintain Austria-Hungary for sixty-six years. Sure, Lombardy and Venice were lost, but on the other hand, Bosnia and Herzegovina were added to the Empire—the terrible tragedy of Mayerling must be explained by the mental derangement of the times—not only do I not believe that the House of Habsburg suffered unusual misfortunes, I reject emphatically such a theory."

I couldn't help smiling at so loyal and determined an expression of his love for the former ruling dynasty. In a way, Prince Clary and my dear friend Edith Riedl had something in common. Because of their personal involvement with Francis Joseph and his house they could see only that which they were led to see. The mystique of the Habsburg charm, the special position of the ruling dynasty, was never in doubt in their minds. Thus, they overlooked some of the *hard realities* of history in the *seemingly inexplicable chain of misfortunes* that beset this family from the very early days. But curses do not simply go away until they are fulfilled.

The legend of the first Habsburg curse is no less real because the "scientific" sources about the family fail to mention it. While the Habsburgs were in power—for over seven hundred years—any reference to such a thing would have been unthinkable in print. And after 1918 no one really cared. Local tradition, especially when it is persistent, is not without evidential value.

My late historian-friend, J. K., never doubted for a moment that the origin of the Habsburg curse, as he had learned it, was essentially true. The second and third Habsburg curses are, of course, well documented. What this combination of maledictions did to the Habsburg family is a matter of record, not speculation.

Nine hundred years after the original curse was uttered, the Habsburgs are reduced to being just another old family. For the past few years their lives have been uneventful and fulfilled. Could it be that the curse found its mark with the death of Emperor Charles I and the loss of the thrones of Austria and Hungary?

The Habsburgs in This Book

(Sons unless otherwise stated)

Guntram the Rich (950 AD)
Lanzelin
Radbot   Werner   Brother-in-
Albert the Rich   (1199)   law   (1096)
Rudolph the Old   (1232)

HABSBURG LINE   LAUFENBURG LINE

Albert the Wise and
   Hedwig   (1240)   Rudolph the Younger
Emperor Rudolph I   (1291)
Emperor Albert I   (1308)
   Brother Rudolph II
Emperor Frederick the
   Handsome   (1330)   John Parricida   (1315)
   And his brothers, Leopold,
   Albert II and Otto
Albert III
   Son of Leopold   (1395)
Albert IV   (1404)
Albert V Better known as
   Emperor Albert II   (1439)
Emperor Frederick III   (1493)
   Cousin to Albert II
Maximilian I   (1519)
Philip the Handsome   (1506)

IMPERIAL LINE

Charles V	(1556)	and Ferdinand I	(1564)
Philip II of Spain	(1598)	Maximilian II	(1576)
Don Carlos	(1568)	Rudolph II	(1612)
Philip III Brother	(1621)	Matthias Brother	(1619)
Philip IV	(1665)	Ferdinand II Cousin	(1637)
Charles II	(1700)	Ferdinand III	(1657)
		Leopold I	(1705)
		Joseph I	(1711)
		Charles VI Brother	(1740)

HABSBURG-LORRAINE

Maria Theresa	(1780)	and Francis I	(1765)
Joseph II	(1790)		
Leopold II Brother	(1792)		
Francis II Later Francis I			
of Austria	(1835)		
Ferdinand I Nephew	(1848)		
Francis Joseph Nephew	(1916)		
Crown Prince Rudolph	(1889)		
Crown Prince Francis			
Ferdinand Nephew	(1914)		
Charles I Grand			
Nephew	(1918, d. 1922)		
Otto	(born 1912)		

Principal Literature Consulted

Edward Cranshaw, *The Habsburgs*
Paul Frischauer, *Die Habsburger*
Otto von Habsburg, *Oesterreich und Europa*
——, *Ein Programm der Freiheit*
——, *Kaiser Franz Josef*
Hugo Hantsch, *Die Geschichte Oesterreichs*, Vol. I
H. G. Koenigsberger, *The Habsburgs and Europe, 1516–1660*
Alexander Lernet-Holenia, *Mayerling*
Count Carl Lonyay, *Rudolph—The Tragedy of Mayerling*
Henry W. Lanier, *He Did Not Die at Mayerling*
Hannes Loderbauer, *Schloss Ort am Traunsee*
Richard Marvin, *The Kennedy Curse*
Gertrude von Schwarzenfeld, *Rudolf II*
Arthur Werner, *Otto von Habsburg*
Adam Wandruszka, *Das Haus Habsburg*
The documents and files of the Austrian State Archives, Vienna
    and
Fritz Hauswirth, *Burgen und Schloesser der Schweiz*, Vol. 3.
Geographisches Lexicon der Schweiz